RAMAKRISHNA-VIVEKANANDA CENTER
OF NEW YORK
17 East 94th Street, New York, N.Y. 10128

PUBLICATIONS

By Swami Nikhilananda

HINDUISM: Its Meaning for the Liberation of the Spirit
HOLY MOTHER: Being the Life of Sri Sarada Devi, Wife
of Sri Ramakrishna and Helpmate in His Mission
MAN IN SEARCH OF IMMORTALITY: Testimonials from
the Hindu Scriptures
VIVEKANANDA: A BIOGRAPHY

Translated by Swami Nikhilananda

THE BHAGAVAD GITA
THE BHAGAVAD GITA (Pocket Edition)
THE GOSPEL OF SRI RAMAKRISHNA
THE GOSPEL OF SRI RAMAKRISHNA (Abridged Edition)
SELF-KNOWLEDGE (Atmabodha)
THE UPANISHADS Volumes I, II, III, and IV

By Swami Vivekananda

INSPIRED TALKS, My Master and Other Writings
JNANA-YOGA
KARMA-YOGA AND BHAKTI-YOGA
RAJA-YOGA

VIVEKANANDA: THE YOGAS AND OTHER WORKS
(Chosen and with a Biography by Swami Nikhilananda)

HINDUISM

ITS MEANING FOR
THE LIBERATION
OF THE SPIRIT

HINDUISM

ITS MEANING FOR
THE LIBERATION
OF THE SPIRIT

BY

SWAMI NIKHILANANDA

RAMAKRISHNA–VIVEKANANDA CENTER
NEW YORK

HINDUISM: ITS MEANING FOR THE
LIBERATION OF THE SPIRIT

*For information address
Ramakrishna-Vivekananda Center
17 East 94th Street,
New York, N.Y. 10128.*

PAPERBACK EDITION 1992

ISBN 0-911206-26-4
Library of Congress catalogue card number: 58-6155

Contents

Acknowledgments

THE AUTHOR wishes to express his gratitude to the University of Hawaii Press, Honolulu, for permission to use material from his article entitled "Concentration and Meditation as Methods in Indian Philosophy," published in *Essays in East-West Philosophy* (1951), in preparing the chapter dealing with raja-yoga; and to the Sri Ramakrishna Committee, Belur Math, Calcutta, for permission to use material from an article by Pramathanath Mukhopadhyaya entitled "Tantra as a Way of Realization," published in *The Cultural Heritage of India* Vol. II (1937), in preparing the chapter dealing with Tantra. He is also grateful to Dr. Nelson S. Bushnell and Brahmachari Yogatmachaitanya for reading the manuscript and making many valuable suggestions for the improvement of the text, and to Mrs. W. E. Bankert and Miss Cora Washburn for typing the manuscript.

Foreword

IN THE following pages I have attempted to give a brief account of Hinduism in both its theoretical and its practical aspects. It is written mainly from the point of view of non-dualism, which, in my opinion, is the highest achievement of India's mystical insight and philosophical speculation, and her real contribution to world culture. Non-dualism preaches the ✓ oneness of existence as ultimate truth. It asserts that knowledge, after revealing the identity of subject and object, can go no further. Hence the truth it preaches is claimed to be the whole truth and therefore free from contradiction, since only a partial truth may be contradicted. For the same reason, non-dualism has no quarrel with any other system, harmonizes conflicting philosophical doctrines, and lends itself to the welfare of all beings.

Explanations of Hinduism which are often incorrect and misleading have been given by non-Hindus. It is almost impossible for an outsider to enter into the spirit of a religion in which he has not been brought up. And the same objection applies to interpretations of Hinduism offered by those who, lacking any real feeling for its teachings, call themselves Hindus by virtue of the mere accident of birth. This book, it is hoped, expresses the beliefs of a good Hindu about his religion and philosophy. It will be seen that the various ideas of Hinduism here presented, about such matters as the nature of God, the soul, creation, ethics, spiritual disciplines, popular religious practices, and interreligious relations, all hang together and give an integrated view of life from its first wandering into the phenomenal world to its attainment of the journey's end.

One often hears it said that Hinduism is responsible for much of the injustice and selfishness in Hindu society. To be sure, injustice and selfishness exist; but to lay the blame for these at the door of the teachings of the Upanishads and the Bhagavad Gita, the main sources of Hinduism, is as unreasonable as to make the teachings of Christ responsible for a lack of humility and consideration for others' rights apparent in avowedly Christian nations. One cannot condemn Hinduism for the present poverty and backwardness of India any more than one can condemn the Sermon on the Mount—with its lofty ideal of forgiveness, non-resistance of evil, and universal love—for the support of war by a militant Christian church. The real culprit is men's distortion or defiance of their own basic religious concepts. Unfortunately, a certain perversity in human nature cooperates with the present organization of society to create a gap between ideals and their application.

Contrary to popular views, Hinduism does not repudiate the world, negate social values, or forbid the enjoyment of legitimate pleasures; it points the way to enduring happiness both here and hereafter, and to the highest good as well. The history of India shows that when the country was spiritually great it was also materially prosperous and culturally creative. Nor is Hinduism opposed to rational thinking. One of the universal prayers of the Hindus supplicates for "clear intellect." Furthermore, the Upanishads exhort students to study both science and super-science, or what they call the "lower knowledge" and the "higher knowledge." With the help of the former a man overcomes poverty, disease, and death, and with the help of the latter he attains to immortality; and it is repeatedly stated in the scriptures that both these forms of knowledge are necessary to "dispel doubts and sever the knots of the heart."

Indian culture was created and supported by certain spiritual concepts, which are discussed in the body of this book. Loyalty to these concepts has preserved Hindu society during many centuries of foreign domination—a domination of the sort that in other countries destroyed the native culture. That India is still alive and dynamic needs no proof; it has been amply demonstrated by her recent successful struggle for independence. One need not cut open the bark of a living tree to see if the sap is running. For more than a century India has been passing through a spiritual renaissance, which has now culminated in her winning of political freedom. Practically all of her national leaders from Ram Mohan Roy to Gandhi—through Vivekananda, Tilak, Aurobindo Ghosh, and Subhas Bose—have championed the cause of Hinduism, though they were stimulated in varying degrees by their contact with the West. Gandhi employed a typical religious discipline to overcome India's foreign rule.

It seems that the very life of India is centred in religion. It is her mission to the world. One cannot understand India without understanding Hinduism. If India gives up religion and takes exclusively to politics, science, and technology to build her future, she will be courting disaster. All of her national activities must be inspired by religion. This seems to be the mandate of India's past.

The whole world faces today the challenge of a secularism brought into focus in the sudden development of science and technology. These have released a power which may demand satisfaction with human blood. But this is not inevitable. The physical sciences, which, like religion, are governed by universal laws, can, if they are animated by certain spiritual ideals, help to build an ideal world. Religions, too, if informed by the scientific spirit of reasoning and experimentation, can rid themselves of superstition and dogmatism. Without the help of technology, many of the cherished ideals of religion, such as the divinity of the soul and human brotherhood, would remain mere abstract theories. The separation of science and religion has been a major tragedy for the human race. The relationship between them may be likened to that of body and soul: the body without a soul is a mere corpse, and the soul without a body, a mere phantom.

The world's malady is spiritual. Suspicion, ill-will, fear, and greed, which have been poisoning human relationships, are the symptoms of an inner sickness. For the world's recovery the root of this sickness must be removed. Religion alone can accomplish the cure by generating in men the power of aggressive goodness necessary to fight aggressive evil. Nowadays, various substitutes for religion are suggested, such as humanism, psychotherapy, ethical conduct, or the apotheosis of the state. But these cannot take the place of religion, which is unique in that it reveals the eternal relationship between the eternal soul and the eternal reality.

As human institutions, all organized faiths have their limitations; these, however, can be corrected through the study of the different religions, not in a spirit of carping criticism but with respect and affection. The great religions of the world, as Toynbee has recently said, echoing the time-honoured Hindu belief, are not competitive but complementary. One religion is not the enemy of another, but all religions are faced today by common enemies: scepticism, atheism, and, perhaps worst of all, serene indifference. Only if the religions of the world stand together will they preserve themselves. In their survival they will help to bring about a new manifestation of the world spirit, for whose sake humanity is patiently bearing its present travail and uncertainty.

NIKHILANANDA

HINDUISM

ITS MEANING FOR
THE LIBERATION
OF THE SPIRIT

I.

The Spirit of Hinduism

HINDUISM is the dominant religion of the vast Indian sub-continent, and since the beginning of its history has profoundly influenced the lives and thoughts of countless millions of the Indian people from cradle to grave. It has left an indelible impress on the entire culture of India: on her philosophy, art, architecture, literature, politics, sociology. Religion gives to a Hindu equanimity of mind in prosperity and adversity, courage to face the problems of his life, and a vision of his ultimate spiritual destiny. Through Buddhism, an offshoot of Hinduism, India has influenced the spiritual culture of Ceylon, Burma, Tibet, China, Japan, Korea, and other countries of Asia, many of which still regard India as their spiritual homeland.

India did not, in the past, develop a national unity, in the political sense, like that enjoyed by the nations of the West. But her people, owing allegiance to common spiritual ideals, have been held together by an intangible religious bond. That is why they did not disintegrate as a nation despite a prolonged foreign domination and other vicissitudes of history. Diversities of ritual and belief, of food and dress, caste and social behaviour, language and politics, have not been able to destroy this deeper spiritual unity. Scratch a modern Hindu and you will find him religious in spite of his veneer of secular upbringing and education.

Through her religion and philosophy India has earned the respect of many thoughtful people of the Western world. To quote the words of Max Muller:

> If one would ask me under what sky the human mind has most fully developed its precious gifts, has scrutinized most profoundly the greatest problems of life, and has, at least for some, provided solutions which deserve to be admired even by those who have studied Plato and Kant, I would indicate India. And if one would ask me which literature would give us back (us Europeans, who have been exclusively fed on Greek and Roman thought, and on that of a Semitic race) the necessary equilibrium in order to make our inner life more perfect, more comprehensive, more universal, in short, more human, a life not only for this life, but for a transformed and eternal life, once again I would indicate India.

Hinduism is not a set of abstract philosophical theories unrelated to life or a congeries of religious dogmas to be accepted with blind faith; it combines both philosophy and religion, reason and faith, and promises to its votaries a direct insight into reality, and the grounds for the acceptance of that insight. Philosophy saved the Hindu from religious bigotry, and religion saved him from the ivory-tower attitude of cold intellectualism. Whenever, in the course of Hinduism's development, religion erred by emphasizing ritual or dogma as the only means to the highest goal, a sound rational philosophy put it on the right path, and whenever intellect claimed the role of sole pathfinder, religion showed the futility of mere discursive reasoning and stressed the importance of worship as a discipline for communion with ultimate reality. Thus not only the seers of the Upanishads, but also Buddha and Sankaracharya (A.D. 788–820) repudiated the claims of the popular religion of their time to be the exclusive means for the realization of the highest good. The author of the Bhagavad Gita as well as Ramanuja (A.D. 1017–1137), Chaitanya (A.D. 1485–1533), and other mystics raised their voices against arid intellectualism. In our own day Ramakrishna (1836–1886) harmonized the apparent conflict between reason and faith. In the Hindu tradition, reason saves the aspiring devotee from avoidable errors and pitfalls, work purifies his heart, meditation creates one-pointedness of mind, love gives him the urge to move forward, faith supports him with courage in the hour of despondency, and the grace of God bestows upon him the final fruit of liberation.

Not being a historical religion like Buddhism, Christianity, or Islam, each of which has been articulated by the teachings of its individual founder, Hinduism baffles all attempts to give it an easy and convenient definition; the truths of the Hindu scriptures, the Vedas, were not formulated by historical persons. Moreover the universal nature of Hinduism frustrates any endeavour to confine it in exact statement; the Vedas preach an impersonal reality as ultimate truth, and not the Personal God, though they make room for such a God and for other divinities.

Hinduism, though based essentially on the teachings of the Vedas, is secondarily derived from the moral and religious precepts of many prophets and saints, philosophers and law-givers, of ancient, medieval, and modern times. It is thus a growing organism daily enriched by new truths, emerging from the experiences of living men and women, which have preserved its vitality and prevented it from being cluttered with lifeless dogmas. But Hinduism's main foundation still remains the Vedas, whose teachings are not the product of human intellect. These scriptures contain eternal truths regarding the nature of ultimate reality, the creation, and the soul and its destiny, which cannot be determined through sense-data and reasoning based upon them. They also tell us about the cosmic divinities, the various heavens, the different courses followed by souls after death, and other similar phenomena beyond the reach of the senses. As timeless as the creation itself, these truths were discovered for the Indian world, and not created, by certain seers who were possessed of rare insight attained through moral disciplines, intense concentration, intellectual acumen, unflagging self-control, and utter non-attachment to transitory pleasures. These seers of truth, both men and women, were called rishis; they lived mostly on the banks of the Indus and the Ganges, in northern India. We know almost nothing about their personal lives, for it was not the person, but the ideas they stood for, that appealed to the ancient Hindus.

According to Hindu philosophers a conclusion regarding a spiritual truth depends for its validity on three factors: the scriptures, reason, and personal experience. An aspirant, with the help of a qualified teacher, should first study the scriptures, which record the spiritual experiences of past seers of truth. Then he must subject the instruction thus received to rigorous reasoning. Finally, after being convinced of the soundness of what he has studied, he must meditate on it and experience it in the depths of contemplation. Neither the Vedas, however, nor reasoning, nor experience can independently create genuine conviction. By depending solely upon the scriptures one becomes dogmatic. Reason, by itself, cannot give certainty, and often it is found that reasoning conceals the rationalizing of a man's desire; he proves what he wants to prove. Personal experience by itself can also be deceptive in that it may project one's own favourite ideas. But when all three factors jointly lead to the same conclusion, one may be reasonably assured of having reached the truth, just as, for instance, a law in the United States of America is accepted as valid when it is approved by the Congress, the Executive, and the Supreme Court. The authority of the Vedas does not depend upon supernatural beings or historical evidence, which may be shaken by science or by new historical discoveries. It is ultimately derived from spiritual experiences which are attainable by every human being.

The Vedas are concerned not only with man's longing for the supreme goal, which has been described as freedom, peace, bliss, or immortality, but also with his more immediate impulse toward material pleasures here on earth and happiness in heaven. The latter represents a universal yearning and can be fulfilled, according to the Vedas, through the help of the gods or superhuman beings, and also through the discharge of social obligations. The interdependence of the gods, men, subhuman creatures, and nature is admitted, the welfare of one being dependent upon the welfare of all. In Vedic times the gods were propitiated by means of oblations offered into the sacrificial fire, which have now been replaced by the ritualistic worship in temples and popular shrines. The sacrifices and similar methods of worship have been described in the ritualistic section of the Vedas, called the Karma-kanda, and the disciplines for freedom in the philosophical section, called the Jnana-kanda, which comprises the Upanishads.

Who are these Vedic gods, known by such names as Prajapati, Indra, Varuna, Yama, and Rudra? Generally speaking, gods occupy exalted positions from which they control the rain, sunshine, the wind, water, fire, death, and other natural phenomena. They are manifestations of the power of Brahman, or ultimate reality, in the phenomenal universe. Some of them also control the activities of the mind, the vital breath, and the sense-organs in the human body, which, being material in nature, would be inert and unconscious were they not animated by Brahman. The ancient Hindus prayed to the gods for longevity, health, children, grandchildren, and material prosperity. The gods were the custodians of the social well-being of men, from whose sacrificial oblations they drew their sustenance; they therefore became annoyed if men violated their social obligations. But a devotee, by worshipping them without any selfish motive, through their grace obtained purity of heart, which helped him in the realization of truth.

The Vedas enjoin it upon all to treat with kindness subhuman beings, such as beasts and birds, which help to promote human happiness. Thus a man's enjoyment of earthly pleasures depends upon his discharge of his duties to the gods, his fellow human beings, and the beasts and birds. The satisfaction derived from a harmonious relationship with other living beings produces inner contentment and opens the gateway to the higher life. But the satisfaction derived from ruthless competition with others, or from unkind treatment of lower creatures, or from indifference to the gods, in the end brings frustration and is without any spiritual significance. The Vedas emphasize the fact that happiness on earth and in heaven is transitory, because it is related to impermanent material objects, and also because it is an effect and can therefore endure only so long as the momentum given by its cause endures. The denizens of heaven eventually must return to earth and continue their apparently interminable round of birth and death in a universe governed by the laws of time, space, and causality. He who is attached to the universe and seeks happiness from it cannot attain to liberation, which is possible only through the knowledge of the self or Brahman, described in the Upanishads.

The secondary scriptures of Hinduism are the various Smritis and Puranas, which give a popular interpretation of the philosophical truths of the Vedas. These secondary scriptures must not contradict the central philosophy of the Vedas described in the Upanishads, but should show how to apply these truths to society and to the individual life, according to the demands of changing times. A distinctive feature of Hinduism is that while it remains utterly loyal to the eternal truths, it admits the need for new dogmas and rituals to suit changing conditions. A medieval dogma cannot satisfy the modern world.

In a sense Hinduism is a complex religion; but complexity is inherent in human nature. People are endowed with different temperaments, tastes, and tendencies. Some want total identity with the Deity, while others wish to preserve their separate identities; some are intellectual, some introspective, some devotional, and some active. Thus disciplines vary. Furthermore, some prefer to contemplate an impersonal spiritual ideal, and some to worship a tangible deity, whether the Personal God or a crude image of clay or stone. Besides, different people emphasize different attributes of God: justice, power, beauty, law, love, peace. These attributes, however, are not contradictory but rather complementary, like the different coloured stones in a mosaic or the different patterns in a tapestry. Hinduism has blended these differences into one comprehensive religio-philosophical system, the keynote of which is unity in diversity. A synthesis of many religions, Hinduism has an irresistible appeal for religious-minded people.

According to the Vedas, ultimate reality is all-pervading, uncreated, self-luminous, eternal spirit, the final cause of the universe, the power behind all tangible forces, the consciousness which animates all conscious beings. This is the central philosophy of the Hindu, and his religion consists of meditation on this spirit and prayer for the guidance of his intellect along the path of virtue and righteousness.

From the philosophical standpoint, Hinduism is non-dualistic, and from the religious standpoint, monotheistic. The Hindu philosophy asserts the essential non-duality of God, soul, and universe, the apparent distinctions being created by names and forms which, from the standpoint of ultimate reality, do not exist. Though the Hindu religion admits of many popular divinities, it regards them as diverse manifestations of the one God. Through them He fulfils the desires of His devotees. The Hindu trinity of Brahma, Vishnu, and Siva represents the three aspects of the Godhead which control the processes of creation, preservation, and destruction respectively. Any one of them is incomplete and illusory without the other two. Through unceasing creation and destruction God preserves the universe. Hindu monotheism does not repudiate the various deities of the different faiths, but includes them as the manifestations of the One.

According to Hinduism, religion is experience and not the mere acceptance of certain time-honoured dogmas or creeds. To know God is to become like God. A man may quote scripture, engage in ritual, perform social service, or pray with regularity, but unless he has realized the divine spirit in his heart, he is still a phenomenal being, a victim of the pairs of opposites. One can experience God as tangibly as "a fruit lying on the palm of one's hand," which means that in this very life a man can suppress his lower nature, manifest his higher nature, and become perfect. Through the experience of God, a man's doubts disappear and "the knots of his heart are cut asunder." By ridding himself of the desires clinging to his heart, a mortal becomes immortal in this very body. That the attainment of immortality is not the prerogative of a chosen few, but the birthright of all, is the conviction of every good Hindu.

The four cardinal principles of Hinduism may be summed up as follows: the non-duality of the Godhead, the divinity of the soul, the unity of existence, and the harmony of religions.

On these four principles the faith of a good Hindu is based. The articles of that faith will be discussed in detail in the succeeding chapters of this book.

Contrary to the opinion held by many both inside and outside India, Hinduism has never condemned a rich and full life in the world or extolled poverty as a virtue in itself—though the case is different with monks, who voluntarily take the vow of mendicancy. Dharma, or righteousness, has been defined as what is conducive to both the enjoyment of legitimate material pleasures and the realization of the highest good, according to people's different stages of evolution. The Upanishads exhort men to enjoy life for a hundred years, giving up greed and possessiveness. It was India's fabulous wealth that invited foreign invaders, from the Greeks to the modern Europeans. Religion has never been the cause of India's poverty; it is indifference to religious precepts that has been largely responsible for her general backwardness. In an ideal society the majority of people should be householders performing their different duties as priests and philosophers, kings and warriors, tradesmen and farmers, and lastly as manual workers, according to their innate aptitudes. Only a minority should be monks, practising renunciation, both external and internal, in order to demonstrate the supremacy of the spirit.

One sees in India a large number of persons wandering about in monastic garb, many of whom are not genuine mendicants. These persons have taken to the monastic life for various reasons. According to the philosophically sound nondualistic interpretation of Vedanta, the knowledge of the nondual Brahman is utterly incompatible with the performance of duties which admit of the triple factors of doer, instrument of action, and result. Hence people have often sought what they thought to be an easy way to the highest knowledge through renunciation of worldly duties. A negative interpretation of the

doctrine of maya is often responsible for the erroneous notion
that the world is unreal. Buddha definitely taught that Nirvana
could be attained only by world-renouncing monks, and his
followers later welcomed people to the monastic life without
much discrimination. Because of the general spirit of renunciation that pervades Hinduism, the monastic life has an irresistible appeal for religious-minded Hindus. A man who cannot
easily earn his livelihood, when dressed as a monk always obtains a few morsels of food from god-fearing and hospitable
householders. Furthermore, on account of the frustrations
caused by prolonged foreign domination, many Hindus have
sought an escape from the exacting demands of life by renouncing the world and making a cult of poverty and as-
ceticism. All this accounts for the presence of numerous monks
in Hindu society. There are, of course, many genuine monks
who, through renunciation of the world, have kept alive the
highest ideals of Hinduism. In recent times Swami Vivekananda gave a new direction to monastic life by supplement-
ing the ideal of renunciation with that of service to humanity,
exhorting monks to work for the uplift of the masses. Heeding
his advice, many individual monks and many monastic or-
ganizations have taken up various social and educational activities to improve the people's condition.

But the general tenor of Hinduism has been to encourage
householders to enjoy material goods without deviating from
the path of righteousness. A Hindu proverb says: "Fortune
in full measure resides in trade and commerce, one half of
that in agriculture, and one half again of that in service to
the government; but the goddess of fortune quickly runs away
from a beggar." The life depicted in the Vedas and Puranas
is a joyous, affirmative, optimistic, and creative life. What is
seen in India today in society and religion is not a true index
of Indian culture.

Religion has always been the backbone of India. During the days of her national misfortune it was religion that saved Hindu society from total disintegration. All through the period of her political decline, saints and mystics have urged her to give up vanity and pride, and cultivate love of men and devotion to God. India listened to their advice and survived. In the history of the world she is perhaps the solitary instance of an ancient nation whose soul could not be destroyed by ruthless conquerors either by force or persuasion, while many younger nations have disappeared after a meteoric display of physical power and glory.

The chapters to come will reveal the various dimensions of Hinduism. Its extent includes the conception of Brahman, or absolute reality, which is the foundation of the moral and spiritual laws that guide the universe, and under whose control the sun, moon, and stars move along their orbits. Its tremendous depth consists in its conception of the soul, subtler than the subtle and greater than the great, guiding the activities of body, sense-organs, and mind. Its breadth appears in its catholic attitude toward all systems of religious and philosophical thought, and in its respect for those who differ from it. One may discover yet a fourth dimension in Hinduism in its realization of the all-embracing unity of animate and inanimate beings: of God, souls, and the universe.

II.

The Godhead and Creation

AS EARLY as Vedic times, the Indo-Aryan thinkers investigated the nature of reality from two levels of experience, one of which may be called the absolute, acosmic, or transcendental level and the other the relative, cosmic, or phenomenal level. At the phenomenal level one perceives the universe of diversity and is aware of one's own individual ego, whereas at the transcendental level all differences merge into an inexplicable non-dual consciousness. Both of these levels of experience are real from their respective standpoints, though what is perceived at one level may be negated at the other.

In the Vedas, reality experienced at the transcendental level is called Brahman. This term denotes a non-dual pure consciousness which pervades the universe and yet remains outside it. Brahman is described as the first principle; from it all things are derived, by it all are supported, and into it all finally disappear. In Brahman alone the apparent differences of the phenomenal world are unified. According to the non-dualistic Vedanta philosophy, Brahman is identical with the self of man, known as atman.

Etymologically, the word *Brahman* denotes an entity whose greatness, powers, or expansion no one can measure. The word *atman* signifies the consciousness in man which experiences gross objects during the waking state, subtle objects during the dream state, and the bliss arising from absence of the duality of subject and object in dreamless sleep.

Let us try to understand the nature of Brahman in both its aspects: transcendental and phenomenal. The Upanishads speak of the transcendental Brahman as devoid of qualifying attributes and indicative marks, and of the phenomenal Brahman as endowed with them. The attributeless Brahman is called the supreme or unconditioned Brahman, and the other the inferior or conditioned Brahman. The supreme Brahman, or pure being, is described by a negative method in such striking passages as: "Not this, not this," or "Where there is duality, as it were, one sees another, but when only the self is all this, how should one see another?" The conditioned Brahman, on the other hand, has been described by such positive statements as: "Whose body is spirit, whose form is light, whose thoughts are true, whose nature is like akasa, from whom all works, all desires, all odours proceed." The Upanishads generally designate the conditioned Brahman by the masculine *He* and the unconditioned Brahman by the neuter *it*.

There is no real conflict between the two Brahmans; for Brahman is one and without a second, and can be regarded either from the phenomenal or from the transcendental point of view. When the sense-perceived world is regarded as real, Brahman is spoken of as its omnipotent and omniscient Creator, Preserver, and Destroyer. But when the world is not perceived to exist, as for instance in a deep meditation, then one experiences Brahman as the unconditioned Absolute; the idea of a Creator, omnipotent and omniscient, becomes irrelevant. One worships the conditioned Brahman in the ordinary state of consciousness; but one loses one's individuality in the experience of the unconditioned Brahman. As we shall see later, the transcendental Brahman appears as the cause of the universe in association with maya, and becomes known as the conditioned Brahman or Brahman with attributes, or by such other epithets as the Lord and the Personal God.

First let us consider the unconditioned Brahman. Indescribable in words, it is indicated by the Vedas as that "from which all speech, together with the mind, turns away, unable to reach it." Ramakrishna has said that all the scriptures and all the statements of holy men have been polluted, as it were, like food that has come in contact with the tongue; Brahman alone remains unpolluted, because it has never come in contact with any tongue. He used to say, further, that he had to come down three levels, so to speak, from the experience of non-duality before he could utter the word *Om,* a holy symbol of Brahman. Experienced as silence, the attributeless Brahman is described as "not that which is conscious of the external (objective) world, nor that which is conscious of the internal (subjective) world, nor that which is conscious of both, nor that which is a mass of sentiency, nor that which is simple consciousness, nor that which is insentient. It is unperceived [by any sense-organ], unrelated [to anything], incomprehensible [to the mind], uninferable, unthinkable, indescribable."

Sometimes the Upanishads ascribe to the unconditioned Brahman irreconcilable attributes in order to deny to it all empirical predicates and indicate that it is totally other than anything we know: "That non-dual Brahman, though never stirring, is swifter than the mind. Though sitting still it travels far; though lying down it goes everywhere." "It is subtler than an atom and greater than the great." The opposing predicates in these passages are ascribed to Brahman in such a manner that they cancel each other, leaving to the mind the idea of an indefinable pure consciousness free of all attributes. Though nothing definite can be predicated of Brahman, yet the search for it is not futile. The Upanishads repeatedly say that its real-

ization is the supreme purpose of life, because it bestows immortality. When Brahman is known all is known.

The unconditioned Brahman is free from the limiting adjuncts of space, time, and causation. In describing Brahman
as infinitely great and infinitely small, the Upanishads only
point out that it is absolutely spaceless. It is "one and infinite:
infinite in the east, infinite in the south, infinite in the west,
infinite in the north, above and below and everywhere infinite. The east and the other directions do not exist for it—no
athwart, no beneath, no above. The supreme Brahman is not
to be fixed; it is unlimited, unborn, not to be reasoned about,
not to be conceived." "It is my self within the heart, smaller
than a corn of rice, smaller than a corn of barley, smaller than
a mustard seed, smaller than a canary seed or the kernel of a
canary seed. It is my self within the heart, greater than the
earth, greater than the sky, greater than heaven, greater than
all these worlds."

The timelessness of the unconditioned Brahman is indicated
by the statement that it is free from the limitations of past,
present, and future. Sometimes it is described as eternal, without beginning or end; sometimes as momentary, involving no
time at all. Brahman is "what they say was, is, and will be."
It is that "at whose feet, rolling on, the year with its days
passes by." "It is like a flash of lightning; it is like a wink of
the eye."

Brahman is independent of causation. The law of cause and
effect operates only in the realm of becoming, or manifestation, and cannot affect pure being. Brahman, according to the
Vedas, is not born; it does not die. But from the level of relative experience Brahman is described as the cause of the universe.

Brahman is unknown and unknowable. To be known, a
thing must be made an object. Brahman, as pure conscious-

ness, is the eternal subject, and therefore cannot be made an object of knowledge. "You cannot see that which is the seer of seeing; you cannot hear that which is the hearer of hearing; you cannot think of that which is the thinker of thought; you cannot know that which is the knower of knowing." Brahman is unknowable for still another reason: it is infinite. What is the infinite? "Where one sees nothing else, hears nothing else, understands nothing else—that is the infinite. Where one sees something else, hears something else, understands something else—that is the finite. The infinite is immortal; the finite, mortal."

Hindu philosophers often describe the unconditioned Brahman as Satchidananda, existence-knowledge-bliss pure and absolute. Existence, knowledge, and bliss are not attributes of reality; they are its very stuff. Pure existence is the same as pure knowledge and pure bliss. The word *existence* indicates that Brahman is not non-existence; the phenomenal universe, which is perceived to exist, cannot have been produced from nothing. But Brahman does not exist as an empirical object— like a pot or a tree, for instance—but as absolute existence, without which material objects would not be perceived to exist. Just as a mirage could not be seen without the desert, which is its unrelated substratum, so also the universe could not be seen if Brahman did not exist as its substratum. When the process of negation is carried on, step by step, there always remains a residuum of existence which cannot be negated. No object, illusory or otherwise, could exist without the foundation of an immutable existence—and that existence is Brahman. Therefore the term *existence,* as applied to Brahman, is to be understood as the negation of both empirical reality and its correlative, unreality. Whether the universe is seen or not seen, Brahman remains as the witness-consciousness. Brahman is often described as the "reality of reality," that is to say, the reality of the tangible world whose empirical reality is accepted.

Brahman is knowledge or intelligence. The identity of Brahman and atman, or the self, has been expressed in the well-known Vedic formula "that thou art." The very conception of atman in the Upanishads implies that it is the knowing subject within us. It is the inner consciousness and the real agent of perception, the senses being mere instruments. Perception, which is a conscious act, is impossible without the presence of a sentient principle, which is atman. "He who says: 'Let me smell this'—he is atman; the nose is the instrument of smelling. He who says: 'Let me utter this'—he is atman; the tongue is the instrument of speaking. He who says: 'Let me hear this'—he is atman; the ear is the instrument of hearing. He who says: 'Let me think this'—he is atman; the mind is his divine eye." "Into him, as eye, all forms are gathered; by the eye he reaches all forms. Into him, as ear, all sounds are gathered; by the ear he reaches all sounds." Because Brahman is identical with atman, Brahman is consciousness, knowledge, light. It is self-luminous and needs no other light to illumine itself. "It is the light of lights; it is that which they know who know the self." All material objects, such as trees, rivers, houses, and forests, are illumined by the sun. But the light that illumines the sun is the light of Brahman. "The sun does not shine there, nor the moon and the stars, nor these lightnings, not to speak of this fire. When he shines everything shines after him; by his light everything is lighted." "The universe is guided by knowledge, it is grounded in knowledge, it is governed by knowledge; knowledge is its foundation. Knowledge is Brahman."

Brahman is bliss because it is knowledge. No real bliss is possible without knowledge. Needless to say, the bliss of Brahman is utterly different from the happiness that a man experi-

ences from agreeable sense-objects; it is characterized by absence
of the subject-object relationship. Worldly happiness is but an
infinitesimal part of the bliss of Brahman. Again, Brahman is
bliss because of the absence of duality in it; friction, fear,
jealousy, secretiveness, and the other evils which plague a
man's daily life arise from consciousness of duality. Brahman
as bliss pervades all objects; that is why there is attraction between husband and wife, parents and children, creature and
creature, God and man. Furthermore, Brahman is bliss because it is infinite. There is no real and enduring joy in the
finite. The bliss of Brahman cannot be measured by any relative standard, human or other. Through the performance of
religious rites and the fulfilment of moral obligations one may
experience, after death, different measures of happiness in
ascending degrees in the different heavenly worlds. But if a
person is completely free from desire and possesses the knowledge of Brahman, he can attain here, before death, the meas-
ureless bliss of Brahman.

To summarize what has been said about the unconditioned
Brahman, or pure being: Brahman is the negation of all attributes and relations. It is beyond time, space, and causality.
Though it is spaceless, without it space could not be conceived;
though it is timeless, without it time could not be conceived;
though it is causeless, without it the universe, bound by the
law of cause and effect, could not be conceived to exist. Only
if one admits the reality of pure being as the unchanging
ground of creation can one understand proximity in space,
succession in time, and interdependence in the chain of cause
and effect. Without the unchanging white screen, one cannot
relate in time and space the disjoined pictures on a cinema
film. Brahman is not a philosophical abstraction, but is more
intimately known than any sense-object. It is Brahman that,
as the inner consciousness, makes the perception of sense-ob-

jects possible. Brahman is the intangible reality that unifies all the discrete objects in the phenomenal universe, making it appear a cosmos and not a chaos. In the Vedas, Brahman is compared to a dike that keeps diverse objects asunder and prevents their clashing together, or again, to a bridge that connects the visible world with the invisible.

From the transcendental standpoint, there exists, therefore, no universe which is other than Brahman. Since Brahman is free from causality, the question of creation does not arise. Nothing is ever produced. Where, on account of ignorance, a man sees names and forms, substance and attributes, causal and other relationships, the knower of reality sees only pure being. To the illumined, nature itself is pure being. Duality being mere illusion, unconditioned pure being is the sole reality.

From the relative standpoint, however, the Vedas concede the reality of the phenomenal universe with all its limitations, and of finite living beings, who need an object of prayer and worship. Obviously the unconditioned Brahman cannot be the object of such prayer or worship; for no relationship whatsoever can be established with it. Moreover, this transcendental non-dualistic position is too lofty for the average mind to grasp. Being a victim of suffering, old age, death, hunger, and thirst, a prey to fear, frustration, and despair, and keenly aware of the various miseries inflicted by the physical body, outer nature, and cosmic forces, a phenomenal creature needs a liberator, a saviour to whom he can pray, a Personal God, benign and compassionate, to whom he can stretch out his hand for succour in the hour of stress and trial. Furthermore, he wants to know the cause and the ultimate goal of the phenomenal universe, which he cannot but accept as real.

The unconditioned Brahman supplies these wants by manifesting itself as the Personal God and also as the Creator,

Preserver, and Destroyer of the universe. By means of its own inscrutable power, called maya, the unconditioned Brahman becomes the conditioned Brahman endowed with attributes— the Personal God, always ready to bestow His grace upon all who pray to Him in distress. It is the conditioned Brahman— described by different religions as the Father in heaven, Jehovah, Allah, or Isvara—by whom the universe has been created, and by whom, after being created, it is sustained, and into whom, in the end, it is absorbed. Creation, preservation, and destruction are the activities of the conditioned Brahman, or the Personal God, which can never affect His transcendental nature; they are mere waves on the surface of the ocean which cannot touch the serenity of its immeasurable depths.

According to the non-dualistic Vedanta, this conditioning of Brahman is not real, but only apparent. The conditioned Brahman is a part of the phenomenal world and appears to be real as long as the universe is regarded as real. In the infinite ocean of pure consciousness, He is the biggest wave. But the unconditioned Brahman and the conditioned Brahman are not two realities. The wave is not essentially different from the ocean; the sea is the same sea, whether it is peaceful or agitated.

Let us now discuss the various aspects of the conditioned Brahman, or Brahman with attributes.

The conditioned Brahman is called Isvara (the Lord), because He is the all-powerful Lord of all, the ruler of the universe. "He, the Lord, is the bestower of blessings, the adorable God." "Under the mighty rule of this Immutable, the sun and moon are held in their positions; under the mighty rule of this Immutable, heaven and earth maintain their positions; under the mighty rule of this Immutable, moments, days, nights, fortnights, months, seasons, and years are held in their respective places. Under the mighty rule of this Immutable, some rivers flow eastward, others flowing westward continue in that direction, and still others keep to their own courses. Under the mighty rule of this Immutable, men praise those that give, the gods depend upon the sacrificer. . . ."

There are two implications to the statement that the conditioned Brahman is the ruler of the universe: First, as law (ritam) He controls the physical and moral aspects of creation and maintains all things in their proper places; thus there is no real confusion in the functioning of the universe. Second, as the inner ruler He guides the activities of all creatures. He dwells within them but is distinct from them; though He is unknown to the creatures, yet He rules them from within.

The conditioned Brahman can inspire great terror, "like a thunderbolt ready to be hurled." "From terror of Him the wind blows; from terror of Him the sun rises; from terror of Him fire and death perform their respective duties." The different deities—the powers that control the various forces of nature—are His manifestations.

The conditioned Brahman is also to be known under the aspect of providence. Under His supervision good and evil produce their respective results. This does not mean that God is the creator of good and evil. As a man departs from God he sees good and evil, just as one sees day and night when one is separated from the sun, which itself is all light. Nor is God affected by good and evil, which function only in the relative world. The Lord is like the light with whose help a good man performs righteous action and a wicked man unrighteous action; the light itself is unattached, though without it no action can be performed. Man reaps the results of his own action. He uses the light of God for good or evil ends according to his inner tendencies created by the action he has performed in past lives. (The question of the soul's first action cannot logically be raised, since from the relative standpoint neither the embodied soul nor time and space have a beginning.) The law of karma, which preserves the order in the world, requires an administrator, just as the laws of the state require a judge to administer them. God is the administrator of the law of karma.

As already stated, from Brahman, that is to say, from the conditioned Brahman, the universe has arisen; in Him the universe, after having arisen, lives, breathes, and moves; and into Him it disappears. During the periods of creation, preservation, and dissolution the universe is not distinct from Brahman. Thus Hinduism gives a spiritual interpretation of the universe as opposed to the materialistic and mechanistic interpretation given by physical science. The creation will be described presently. Brahman, as the inmost essence of things, preserves them all. "He indeed is the God who pervades all regions: He is the first-born and He is the womb. He has been born and will be born. He stands behind all persons, looking everywhere. The God who is in fire, the God who is in water, the God who has entered into the world, the God who is in plants, the God who is in trees—adoration to that God, adoration!" In anticipation of fuller discussion, it should be noted here briefly that the philosophy of the Upanishads is not pantheistic, though Hindu philosophers have described the creation in terms of pantheism, theism, or realism to suit different levels of understanding.

Brahman is the womb into which the universe returns. Hence He is called the Destroyer. Hindu philosophers have formulated a doctrine of cycles to explain the unceasing process of creation and destruction, or more precisely, of manifestation and non-manifestation. This process of manifestation and non-manifestation has been poetically described in the Vedas as the breathing of Brahman. When He exhales, the universe of names and forms appears, and when He inhales, it disappears.

Hinduism does not accept the theory of creation out of nothing at a particular point of time.

Brahman is the Saviour. It is maya, His inscrutable power, that has cast a spell upon the ignorant and made them forget their true, divine nature. When by God's grace this maya is removed, a man attains liberation. "The non-dual Ensnarer rules by His powers. Remaining one and the same, He rules by His powers all the worlds during their manifestation and continued existence. They who know this become immortal." The seers of the Upanishads incessantly prayed that they might be led from the unreal to the real, from darkness to light, and from death to immortality. "O Lord, let Thy gracious face protect me for ever." "The Lord, the Giver of blessings, the adorable God—by revering Him one attains eternal peace." An aspirant seeking enlightenment and conscious of his many weaknesses and limitations feels the need for protection, guidance, and grace. "He, the omniscient Lord, the Creator of the gods and the bestower of their powers, the Support of the universe, He who in the beginning gave birth to the Cosmic Mind—may He endow us with clear intellect." "The wise, by the grace of the Creator, behold the Lord, majestic and desireless, and become free from grief."

Let us now briefly consider the Hindu view of creation. As already stated, from the transcendental standpoint there exists no universe independent of Brahman, or pure being. Since no real change can be imagined in pure being, the question of creation does not arise. As a great non-dualistic philosopher has said: "There is neither creation nor destruction, neither a struggling nor a bound soul, neither a seeker after liberation nor a liberated one—this is the ultimate truth." Where, under the spell of illusion created by a mirage, a man sees water or the reflection of trees, the enlightened person sees only the desert. All the water of the mirage cannot moisten a grain of sand in the desert. But the universe of names and forms is a fact to the average person, as are pleasure and pain, good and evil, and the other pairs of opposites. Hence the Vedic philosophers felt the need of conceding a relative reality to the phenomenal universe and have offered various statements regarding the creation. The aim of these statements is not, however, to assert the reality of the creation but to indicate the sole existence of non-dual pure being by showing that the phenomenal universe is merely phenomenal.

The problem of the relationship between the unconditioned Brahman and the phenomenal universe can never be completely solved; for such a solution is excluded by the very constitution of man's intellect, which functions only in the domain of relativity. Further, a relationship can be imagined only between two existing entities; but pure being and the phenomenal universe are not perceived to coexist. Because when the one is seen the other disappears, the problem of their relationship baffles human reasoning. Any statement about the creation is figurative, and the Vedas give different descriptions of it so that the mind may understand, by easy stages, that in reality there has been no creation at all.

Here is one vivid description of the creation of living beings given in the Upanishads:

In the beginning this universe was Brahman alone, in the shape of a person. He reflected and saw nothing but Himself. He first said: "I am He." Therefore He came to be known by the name I (Aham). Hence, even now, when a person is addressed, he first says: "It is I," and then repeats whatever other name he may have. He (Brahman) was afraid. Therefore people still are afraid when alone. He thought: "Since there is nothing but Myself, what am I afraid of?" Thereupon His fears were gone; for what was there to fear? Assuredly, it is from a second thing that fear arises. He (Brahman) was not happy. Therefore a person, even today, is not happy when alone. He desired a mate. He became the size of a man and wife in close embrace. He divided His body in two; from that division arose husband and wife. Therefore the body, before one accepts a wife, is half of oneself, like the half of a split pea. Therefore this space is indeed filled by the wife. He was united with her. From that union human beings were born. She reflected: "How can He unite with me after having produced me from Himself? Well, let me hide myself." She became a cow, the other became a bull and was united with her; from that union cattle were born. The one became a mare, the other became a stallion; the one became a she-ass, the other became a he-ass and was united with her; from that union one-hoofed animals were born. The one became a she-goat, the other became a he-goat; the one became a ewe, the other became a ram and was united with her; from that union goats and sheep were born. Thus, indeed, He produced everything that exists in pairs, down to the ants.

It should be understood, however, that when Brahman created a man and wife in order to enjoy happiness, He did not do away with His own self, but remained as He was; being one whose resolves always come true, He projected from Himself another body of the size of a man and wife. Such a phenomenon is called maya. On account of maya, one entity appears to become another without losing its own nature, just as the desert appears to be a mirage.

Regarding the creation of the universe, the Upanishads say that as the hair and nails grow on a living person, as the threads come out of a spider, as sparks fly from a burning fire, as melodies issue from a flute, or as waves rise on the ocean, so also has the universe come from Brahman. Through all these illustrations the idea conveyed is that the universe is nothing but Brahman. Thus Brahman is present in the creation, not in part, but undivided, completely, and as a whole.

Even though the *fact* of the phenomenal universe is conceded,
from the standpoint of Brahman the *act* of creation is denied.

Brahman projects the universe without any effort or outside
compulsion, as suggested by the illustration of exhalation and
inhalation. The creation is sometimes described as the lila, the
sport of Brahman, who creates the universe out of sheer sportive pleasure from the very fullness of His nature. The Upanishads say that all creatures are born from bliss, after being
born are sustained by bliss, and in the end enter into bliss. If
that be so, why do we suffer and why is there evil? It is when
we forget Brahman that we experience suffering. Or the creation may be likened to a play on the stage: pain and pleasure
are both part of this divine play. Saint and sinner, king and
beggar, philosopher and idiot, the pious man and the villain,
war and peace, cruelty and charity, bloodshed and compassion
—all are necessary to enrich the play. But the tigers and lions
one sometimes sees on the stage are muzzled; they make the
gesture of inflicting injury, but they cannot really hurt anyone.
What happens in the physical world cannot injure the spirit
in man. The idea of play suggests that a man need not go on
playing his part if he is tired of it; he can quit at any moment.
Hindu philosophers are willing to accept any explanation of
creation, modern or ancient, provided that such an explanation shows the way to the realization of the ultimate oneness
of God, man, and the universe.

Vedanta philosophy often uses the word *maya* to describe
the creation. When it says that the universe is maya, it is only
stating a fact, namely, that the non-dual Brahman appears
inexplicably as another entity: the universe of names and
forms. When a snake is seen in place of a rope, the phenomenon may be described as maya; this, however, does not imply
any explanation of how or why the rope should appear as the
snake, because the rope never really became the snake. It

states only an empirical fact. One can try to understand maya through an illustration from modern science. When a man speaks of a stone as a solid substance, he is only describing an empirical fact; a physicist regards the same stone as a mass of whirling particles or electrical charges. Somehow these intangible particles or charges appear as the solid stone; Vedanta would describe this phenomenon as maya. In the same sense the whole creation is maya. The finite mind, which itself is a product of maya, cannot understand maya's true nature. Yet recognition of the mind's inability to understand this singular phenomenon on account of which non-dual pure being appears as the manifold universe is not an admission of defeat on the part of human intelligence. It only shows that a profound mystery reigns at the heart of reality, a mystery which cannot be fathomed by the intellect. When one rids oneself of maya one sees the universe as pure being.

Vedantist philosophers describe maya as the power of Brahman, dwelling in Brahman itself and non-different from it. Maya is regarded as beginningless, because no beginning in time can be postulated; but maya disappears when one obtains the direct knowledge of Brahman. Further, it is compounded of three gunas, which are its very stuff. The three gunas are, as it were, the three strands which constitute the rope of maya with which men become bound to the phenomenal world. Present in varying degrees in all objects, gross and subtle, including the mind, intellect, and ego, the gunas are known as sattva, rajas, and tamas. Rajas and tamas have opposing characteristics, while sattva strikes a balance between the two. The principal trait of rajas is energy, whose visible effect is seen in ceaseless activity. Rajas creates attachment and suffering. Tamas manifests itself as inactivity, dullness, inadvertence, and stupidity. It is the mother of delusion and represents the veiling-power of maya. Sattva manifests itself as the spiritual

Sattva [margin annotation]

qualities, and is characterized by balance. Though these gunas
are present in everything, sometimes one preponderates and
sometimes another. Anyone attached to the gunas is not free.
The conditioned Brahman, though associated with the gunas,
keeps them under control; with the help of rajas, sattva, and
tamas, respectively, He creates, preserves, and destroys the
universe. Pure being alone is untouched by the gunas.

In the course of the development of Hindu thought, the
meaning of the word *maya* has undergone many changes.
Thus one Upanishad speaks of maya as the magical power of
the Lord by means of which He projects the universe, like a
magician producing two or more coins from one. Another
meaning is the veiling-power of the Lord by which His true
nature becomes concealed. Gradually the word assumed a
more negative and sinister significance. Especially under the
influence of Buddhism, reality was totally denied to the world,
which was regarded as an abode of suffering and evil; to run
away from it was the path to salvation. This development occurred when Indian philosophy had lost its creative spirit and
scholars became preoccupied with writing commentaries on
the ancient texts, on which further commentaries were written
by other scholars. The emphasis on the negative aspect of maya
is one of the reasons for India's present backwardness in the
modern sciences. Since the world was illusory and ultimately
non-existent, some orthodox scholars argued, nothing could be
gained by investigating it or improving it. But science, and
consequently technology, cannot develop without a positive
attitude toward nature.

Christian thinkers in Europe, during the medieval period,
saw the revelation of God not only in the scriptures and in
mystical experience, but in nature as well. They showed a
profound respect for nature, and this, together with their zeal
for precision, gave an impetus to the development of modern

physical science. Even today a sort of mystical urge impels the scientist in his quest to understand the nature of the physical universe. A similar respect for phenomena existed in Vedic times. When one reads the hymns addressed to the dawn, the sun, and other natural phenomena, one forms an idea of the wonder and joy aroused in the minds of the Vedic Hindus while they contemplated nature. In the Vedas great emphasis was laid on the affirmative and optimistic view of life as opposed to the negative and ascetic view which received unnecessary emphasis during the later period. The doubts of the heart cannot be completely resolved unless one has acquired the knowledge of both the universe and Brahman. As originally conceived, the doctrine of maya was not one of pessimism, but only a statement of fact regarding the universe, and indicated the inability of the finite mind to understand the infinite.

In modern times, Ramakrishna worshipped maya as the Divine Mother, who holds in Her womb all living beings; who, like a mother, supports them after creating them; and who, at the end of the cycle, withdraws them unto Herself. He taught that Brahman and maya are non-different, like fire and its power to burn. If you accept the one, you must accept the other. If you see the fire, you must recognize its power to burn. Ramakrishna exhorted his devotees to regard maya as the Divine Mother. Bondage and liberation, he taught, are both of Her making. By Her inscrutable power people become entangled in the world, and again through Her grace they attain liberation. Ramakrishna did not defy or repudiate maya, but approached it with reverence, worshipped it, and through its grace attained to the highest knowledge.

According to Vedanta philosophy, when there is an equilibrium of the three gunas the universe remains in a state of non-manifestation or dissolution; and when that equilibrium is disturbed, on account of the preponderance of one guna or another, there takes place the creation of the material universe. The first element to evolve at the beginning of a cycle is akasa, which is usually but incorrectly translated as ether, space, or sky. Akasa is the intangible material substance that pervades the whole universe. Its existence was postulated because the atmosphere fills only a fraction of the universe, and also because nature abhors a vacuum. Gradually four other elements, namely, air, fire, water, and earth, become manifest; these five elements are not, however, what we perceive with our sense-organs. At first subtle, they become gross by means of a peculiar process of combination. From the gross and subtle elements are produced physical objects, the body, the senses, the mind, the intellect, the mind-stuff, and the ego. Vedanta speaks of five elements only, because from the standpoint of sense-perception there are only five elemental objects in the universe, namely, sound, touch, form, taste, and smell. The unique characteristic of subtle akasa is sound; of subtle air, touch; of subtle fire, form; of subtle water, taste; and of subtle earth, smell.

Maya, which is not essentially different from Brahman, is the material cause, and Brahman, as pure intelligence, is the efficient cause of the universe. After projecting all material forms, Brahman enters into them as life and consciousness and animates them. Thus Brahman, which is transcendental, becomes immanent in the universe.

A unique manifestation of the conditioned Brahman is the avatara, or incarnation of God. Divine incarnation is recognized by both Christianity and Hinduism—with the important difference that according to Christianity the incarnation is limited to one historical personage, whereas Hinduism does not impose any limitation of time or place. God incarnates Himself to fulfil a cosmic need whenever such a need arises.

But an incarnation is different from a saint in that he is endowed with the power of redemption. To paraphrase what Sankaracharya, the great mystical philosopher of India, wrote about the advent of the God-man, in the introduction to his commentary on the Bhagavad Gita:

After people have practised religion for a long time, lust arises among them, discrimination and wisdom decline, and unrighteousness begins to outweigh righteousness. Then, when unrighteousness prevails in the world, the Lord, the First Creator, wishing to ensure the continuance of the universe, incarnates Himself, in part, as a man. He, the eternal possessor of knowledge, sovereignty, power, strength, energy, and vigour, brings under His control maya, the primordial nature characterized by the three gunas. And then, through that maya, He is seen as though born, as though endowed with a body, and as though showing compassion to men; for He is in reality unborn, unchanging, the Lord of all created beings, and by nature eternal, pure, illumined, and free.

Subtle spiritual truths are expressed through a God-man that they may be grasped by the average man of the world. The eternal voice—to use an illustration given by Toynbee—tunes itself to its present audience's receiving set; otherwise it cannot be picked up.

To summarize the implications of the present chapter: Brahman, or ultimate reality, is pure being, unknown and unknowable to the senses and the mind. The conditioned Brahman is the highest expression of this reality in the phenomenal universe. Knowledge of pure being is called the higher knowledge, and knowledge of the universe, the lower knowledge. The higher knowledge brings about immediate liberation from the bondage of time, space, and causality. The lower knowledge is not, however, to be despised; as long as a man is conscious of the ego and the outside world, he must cultivate it.

He who, still conscious of his obligations and responsibilities, follows the way of the impersonal Brahman courts misery. It is the conditioned Brahman that is worshipped in the various religions as the Personal God. To the earnest devotee who wants to see His impersonal form, He reveals that form by removing the veil created by His own maya. Maya cannot delude the knower of pure being. To him everything—even maya—is Brahman. Whether contemplating the Absolute or participating in the activities of the relative universe, the illumined sage is conscious of Brahman alone. Brahman exists everywhere—in names and forms, good and evil, pain and pleasure, life and death—both here and hereafter.

We have discussed God and the creation from the standpoint of non-dualism, which, as the perennial philosophy of India, has a significant message for the modern world. It provides men with a spiritual interpretation of the universe and a humane view of society. The picture of a ruthless universe, in which the strong devour the weak and survival is assured only to the successful aggressor, is replaced by a kindlier view, in which all human beings are recognized as interdependent, and cooperation and willing sacrifice sweeten human relationships. Under its influence the ethical virtues are no longer dictated by self-interest, either crude or enlightened, but become natural patterns of human behaviour. In the doctrine of non-dualism is found the real explanation of the great commandment to love one's neighbour as oneself; for one's neighbour is oneself. This concept of neighbourliness goes beyond common religious, economic, or political affiliations and embraces the whole of humanity, nay, the creation itself. Unless inspired by charity and goodwill, technological knowledge may become a dangerous monster which will not shrink from the destruction of mankind. Unless treated with gentleness, even inanimate nature withholds its blessings from humanity.

The philosophy of non-dualism can bind up the wounds inflicted on a society made loveless by too much emphasis on the separation between man and man. To a suspicious humanity it can restore mutual faith among nations, without which an enduring peace is impossible. In a non-dualistic world a man may rest fearless of his fellow men; for in the light of non-dualism he can readily understand that the killer and the killed, the exploiter and the exploited, the hater and the hated, are not essentially different, and that a man's ill-will must ultimately return to its source. In a non-dualistic society secretiveness does not poison human relationships, and all men are regarded as members of a common family. Non-dualism rejects the idea of separate ethical codes: one for the chosen people and another for the common breed outside the law. A divided ethics has always been a source of discontent, friction, and war.

The philosophy of non-dualism, emphasizing the potential divinity of every human being, bids us show respect to all men, despite their outward differences of colour, creed, economic or social position, and nationality. The concept of the soul's divinity is the spiritual foundation of freedom and democracy.

The philosophy of non-dualism promotes the harmony of religions. Devotees of a Personal God often become narrowminded, regarding themselves as the chosen people. The chosen people cherish toward outsiders the same attitude as the Personal God of the former cherishes toward the deities of the latter; that is to say, they regard themselves as superior. On account of this sense of superiority, they claim special privileges in the world, and along with it the responsibility to redeem erring souls. Such an attitude has been responsible for many quarrels and wars between diverse religions. According to the philosophy of non-dualism, it is pure being which, from the phenomenal standpoint, is regarded as the Personal God and worshipped under different names by the devotees of the different religions.

From the standpoint of non-dualism one sees that all forms of knowledge—scientific, religious, philosophical, or aesthetic —open on the horizon of the Infinite. There is no real division between science and religion; the same law functions in both fields; when operating in the physical world it is called scientific law, and when operating in the spiritual world it is called spiritual law. Scientific law is discovered through reason based on sense-data; spiritual law, through introspection acquired through self-control, non-attachment, and contemplation. Both reason and spiritual intuition, however, are faculties of one and the same mind.

The philosophy of non-dualism gives a spiritual intepretation to life in the light of which man's thought and action receive new dignity and unique meaning.

III.

The Soul and Its Destiny

AS IT does with the Godhead and the universe, the Vedanta philosophy discusses the nature of the soul from two standpoints: absolute or transcendental, and relative or phenomenal. From the absolute standpoint the soul is non-dual, immortal, ever pure, ever free, ever illumined, and one with Brahman. It is untouched by hunger and thirst, good and evil, pain and pleasure, birth and death, and the other pairs of opposites. That is the soul's true nature, the realization of which is the goal of a man's spiritual aspiration and striving. From this absolute standpoint, the soul is called the paramatma or supreme soul.

But from the relative standpoint, the Vedanta philosophy admits the existence of a multitude of individual souls, called jivatmas, and distinguishes them from the supreme soul. Attached to the body, the individual soul is a victim of the pairs of opposites. Entangled in the world, it seeks deliverance from the eternal round of birth and death, and with that end in view studies the scriptures and practises spiritual disciplines under the guidance of a qualified teacher.

When the individual soul becomes aware of its divine nature, it no longer has to practise morality or obey religious injunctions, whose aim is to enable the aspirant still attached to the world to rid himself of lust, greed, anger, egotism, and a narrow view of life. But during the embodied state, if a person sees the distinction between good and evil, he should shun the evil and follow the good.

As the pure Brahman in association with maya becomes the conditioned Brahman, or Isvara (the Personal God), so also in association with the same maya, it becomes the individual soul or jiva. Though both Isvara and jiva are manifestations of Brahman on the relative plane, the difference between them is vast. They are as different from each other as the sun from a glow-worm, or Mount Everest from a mustard seed. This difference is the result of the fact that Isvara keeps maya under His control whereas the jiva is under maya's control. Under the control of maya, the jiva forgets its real nature, but Isvara, with the help of maya, creates, preserves, and destroys the universe. Isvara despite His phenomenal nature, freely moves in His creation, like a spider on its web, whereas the jiva is imprisoned in the world, like a silkworm in its cocoon. The jiva is the worshipper, and Isvara, as the Personal God, is the object of worship. This difference between the jiva and Isvara must be maintained so long as one is conscious of names and forms, as must the difference between a clay lion and a clay mouse. The same lion and mouse, when reduced to clay, lose their differences; likewise, in the ultimate non-dualistic realization, both jiva and Isvara become one in Brahman.

The Upanishads speak of two souls, as it were, dwelling side by side in a man: the real soul and the individual or apparent soul. They are described as two birds, of similar plumage, inseparable friends, which cling to the same tree, one of them eating the fruit, and the other looking on without eating. The apparent soul experiences pain and pleasure as the result of his own actions, good and evil, and is bewildered by its impotence. But the real soul is serene and undisturbed, because it is not attached to the world. When the apparent soul realizes its oneness with the supreme soul its grief passes away. This oneness of the two souls has been stated by such Vedic statements as "That thou art," "This self is Brahman," "I am He," "Brahman is consciousness."

The supreme soul, as we have seen, assumes through maya a body and becomes finite and individualized; but this individualization is neither final nor real. The jiva, impelled by the good and evil fruits of its actions, assumes diverse bodies, follows an upward or a downward course, and roams about overcome by the pairs of opposites, though all the while, "its immortal self remains unattached, like a drop of water on a lotus leaf." Under the control of the three gunas, which constitute maya, it cherishes various desires and fetters itself by its own actions. This is the nature of the jiva or phenomenal soul.

The jiva is associated with the sense-organs, the mind, and the prana, or vital breath. There are ten sense-organs, all subordinate to the mind as the central organ: five organs of perception and five of action. The former comprise the ears, the nose, the organ of taste, the skin, and the eyes; the latter, the hands, the feet, the organ of speech, and the organs of evacuation and generation. The real sense-organ—the eye, for instance—is not the tangible outer organ, nor the nerve which connects it with the brain, but is a fine organ which is not destroyed at death. The sense-organs do not function in sleep, being gathered into the mind.

The mind is the inner organ and consists of such functions as "desire, deliberation, doubt, faith, want of faith, patience, impatience, shame, intelligence, and fear." The impressions carried by the organs of perception are shaped by the mind into ideas; for "we see only with the mind, hear with the mind." Further, the mind changes the ideas into resolutions of the will. One part of the mind, called the manas, creates doubt. There are three other parts of the mind: the intellect (buddhi), which makes decisions, the chitta, which is the storehouse of memory, and the ego (aham), which creates I-consciousness.

The prana, or vital breath, active both in waking and in sleep, keeps the body alive. It has five separate functions, namely, controlling of the breath, carrying downward unassimilated food and drink, pervading the body, ejecting the contents of the stomach through the mouth or conducting the soul from the body at the time of death, and carrying nutrition to every part of the body.

The five organs of action, the five organs of perception, the five pranas, the mind, and the intellect constitute the subtle body of the jiva, which accompanies the individual soul after death, when the gross body is destroyed. The subtle body is the abode of the karma or impressions left by action, determining the nature of the new body and mind when the soul is reborn. "As the jiva does and acts, so it becomes; by doing good it becomes good and by doing evil it becomes evil—it becomes virtuous through good deeds and vicious through evil deeds." Besides the gross and the subtle body, the jiva possesses a causal body which functions during deep sleep. Into the undifferentiated consciousness associated with the causal body, the experiences of waking and dreaming disappear, and out of it they emerge again.

The Vedanta philosophy describes at great length the distinction between the "seer" and the "seen," also known as the subject and the object, the ego and the non-ego. The seer is the perceiver, identical with the subject and the ego, and is conscious and intelligent by nature. The seen is what is perceived, identical with the object and the non-ego, and is insentient by nature. Thus, the seer and the seen are mutually opposed, like light and darkness. Yet it is a matter of common experience that in everyday practical life people do not distinguish between the two, but through ignorance superimpose the attributes of the one upon the other: the subject is confused with the object and *vice versa*. This confusion, observable in a person's daily thought and action, is expressed by such common statements as "This is I," "This is mine," whereby he identifies the "I" or the subject, which is by nature pure consciousness, with such material objects as the body, the senses, the mind, house, country, or other material objects. Furthermore, on account of the same ignorance, he associates the seer or the eternal self with such characteristics of the body as birth, growth, disease, and death; and this confusion is expressed by such statements as "I am born," "I am growing," "I am ill," or "I am dying." Discrimination between the seer and the seen is the prerequisite for knowledge of the self. The seer is the unchangeable and homogeneous consciousness or knowing principle, the subject and the real ego. The seen is what is perceived; it is matter, multiple and changeable.

It is by virtue of its non-dual nature that the seer perceives an object. The eye sees the diversity of colour and shape in the outer world because it is, relatively speaking, one and unchanging. In turn, the mind—relatively speaking, one—is the perceiver of such changing characteristics of the eye as blindness, dullness, or keenness. Finally, the mind itself—endowed with such characteristics as desire, doubt, determination, fear, and fearlessness—is an object perceived by the self or consciousness, because the latter is one and without a second. This consciousness is free from all such changes as birth, growth, decay, or death. If it possessed those attributes, there would have to be someone as their perceiver. Who would that perceiver be? Another self or consciousness? And who would the perceiver of the second consciousness be? The inquiry ends in an infinite regress. The existence of the self or consciousness cannot be an object of doubt, because the doubter himself is that consciousness. The self cannot be denied, because the denier himself is that self or consciousness. The presence of an irrefragable self or consciousness is assumed in all acts of thinking. Vedanta therefore states that all entities—from the gross, tangible objects in the outer world to the body, senses, and mind—belong to the category of the "seen" or the object, and are insentient and changing. The self or consciousness, which is the true "seer" or subject, is unchanging intelligence, and can never be imagined to be non-existent. The Upanishads emphatically declare that there cannot be an absence of knowledge in the knower. Consciousness is the very stuff of the knower: atman in man and Brahman in the universe are completely identical.

The method by which a Vedantist realizes the illusory nature of the phenomenal world is called adhyaropa, and that by which he rids himself of this illusion and arrives at the knowledge of Brahman is called apavada. By adhyaropa it is explained how, on account of illusory superimposition which is the result of ignorance, one thing appears as another and the properties of the one are attributed to the other. Thus the idea of a snake is falsely superimposed upon a rope and the characteristics of the former are attributed to the latter. In the same manner the idea of body, senses, and mind, associated with the non-self, is falsely superimposed upon the self, and the self, which is of the nature of pure consciousness, appears as a jiva, or phenomenal being, subject to the various limitations of the physical world. Through the same inscrutable ignorance, the attributes of the self are superimposed upon the non-self, and the non-self appears to be conscious, intelligent, and full of bliss. Because of this ignorance, again, the universe of names and forms appears to have reality, a characteristic which actually belongs to Brahman.

Apavada is the method by which one negates, through dis-

crimination, the attributes erroneously superimposed, and realizes the true nature of a thing. Thus, by negating the attributes
of the illusory snake one discovers the true nature of the rope,
by negating the attributes of the non-self one discovers the true
nature of the self, and by negating the attributes of the relative
world one discovers the true nature of Brahman. It should be
remembered that the attributes falsely superimposed upon a
thing can never affect its true nature. As the illusory snake
cannot change the nature of the rope, so the superimposed
attributes of birth and death, and pain and pleasure, cannot
in any way change the true nature of the self. Reality cannot
be affected by appearance.

Vedanta analyses the non-self into five sheaths or kosas.
These are the gross physical sheath, the sheath of the prana
or vital breath, the sheath of the mind, the sheath of the intellect, and the sheath of bliss. They are called sheaths, because, like a sheath concealing an object, they conceal the self.
These sheaths are described as being one inside another, the
physical sheath being the outermost and the sheath of bliss the
innermost. The gross sheath contains within it the finer, and
the finer sheath permeates the grosser. Thus, when it is said
that the sheath of the vital breath is inside the gross physical
sheath, it really means that the former, which is finer than the
latter, permeates it. Atman is the finest entity. It is inside all
the sheaths and permeates them all. The effulgence of atman
shines through all the sheaths, though in varying degrees according to their density. Thus the sheath of intelligence reveals
more of the luminosity of atman than the gross physical sheath.

Through ignorance, persistent and stubborn, a man identifies the self with one or more of the sheaths. Vedantic philosophers take considerable pains to describe their unreal nature,
and exhort spiritual seekers to cultivate detachment from them

in order to realize the true glory of the self. Let us try to understand the nature and attributes of the different sheaths.

The gross physical sheath, made of gross matter, is the physical body consisting of flesh, bones, blood, and other physical elements. Non-existent prior to birth and subsequent to death, it subsists on food. Changeable by nature, its existence is transitory and its virtues are ephemeral. Therefore the body cannot be the self, though the ignorant identify it with the self. As long as a man does not give up this false identification, he cannot transcend death or experience the bliss of freedom, no matter how erudite he be in philosophy or science. But the body, if regarded as an instrument, can be a help to the self, just as a house is helpful to one who dwells in it, or a horse is helpful to its rider. Through the help of the physical body one practises spiritual disciplines and transcends ignorance.

The sheath of the prana, or vital breath, is finer than the physical sheath and impels the latter to action. Consisting of the five pranas, it enters the body at the time of conception, leaves it at the moment of death, and produces the feelings of hunger and thirst. Insentient and limited, the sheath of the vital breath cannot be the self, the omnipresent and all-seeing witness.

The sheath of the mind, finer than the sheath of the prana, creates the notion of the diversity of ego and non-ego, of names and forms. The phenomenal world is perceived to exist because of the mind, which is a product of ignorance. The mind, agitated by desires, becomes aware of sense-objects, gross and fine, enjoys them, and becomes attached to them. Differences of caste and social position, as well as the notions of action, means, and end, exist in the mind alone. Swayed by passion, greed, and anger, the mind creates bondage, and freed from them, it shows the way to liberation. The purification of the mind, which is attained through the practice of discrimination and dispassion, is the goal of spiritual discipline. In the pure mind one sees the reflection of the self. The sheath of the mind, consisting of fine material particles, cannot, however, be the self, because it has a beginning and an end, is subject to change, and is characterized by pain and pleasure.

The sheath of the intellect is insentient because the intellect itself is an organ. It appears intelligent and conscious on account of its reflecting the intelligence of the self. This reflection is called the jiva, or individualized soul, which migrates from one body to another, and whose chief characteristic is I-consciousness. Identified with the sheath of the intellect, the self experiences the good and evil of the phenomenal life. The jivahood assumed by the self is without a beginning, just as the ignorance which creates it is without a beginning. The dream-ego does not know the beginning of a dream and accepts the dream as being without a beginning. But when ignorance is destroyed by right knowledge, all such notions as the jivahood of the self and its birth and death cease to exist, just as the dream ego functioning in sleep vanishes when the dreamer awakes. The false superimposition which accounts for the individualized jiva can be destroyed only by the right knowledge of Brahman and not by any other means, such as ritualistic worship, study of the scriptures, or philanthropy.

Finer than the sheath of the intellect is the sheath of bliss, which is not to be confused with the bliss of Brahman because it is stimulated by external factors. It is experienced when one is deeply absorbed in music or art, or when one reaps the fruit of a good deed. But a full functioning of the sheath of bliss is felt in dreamless sleep, from which one awakes with a feeling of happiness and relaxation. Ignorance, nevertheless, persists in deep sleep. This may be known from the fact that whereas the self is omniscient, the person in deep sleep is aware neither of himself nor of the outside world. From the sheath of bliss, a man returns, without a real change of nature, to the world of the pairs of opposites; but the knowledge of the supreme spirit is accompanied by a total transformation of character.

The five sheaths here described, all modifications of prakriti or primordial matter and unreal in themselves, appear to be real because atman is their substratum, as a mirage appears to be real because the desert is its substratum. When the aspirant ceases from identifying himself with the sheaths or with any other modifications of ignorance, the true glory of atman is revealed to him.

Atman is the light that shines through prakriti or matter and is the witness of the experiences of the states of waking, dreaming, and deep sleep. Let us now briefly consider these three states of the jiva's phenomenal experience, which are discussed by the major Upanishads and other Vedantic scriptures in order to lead to right knowledge of the self. Knowledge is based upon experience. Partial experience gives partial knowledge, and total experience, total knowledge. Not one of the three states of waking, dreaming, and deep sleep reveals, by itself, the true nature of the soul, which is called turiya or the fourth. This turiya is the detached witness of the three states and also permeates them. It may be noted here that the physical sciences based upon the experience of the waking state alone, and certain forms of psychoanalysis investigating dreams, and the doctrine of nihilism stressing the absence of empirical knowledge as experienced in dreamless sleep, all yield only partial knowledge.

During the waking state, atman experiences the physical world in common with all men, using the sense-organs as instruments of perception. From the waking standpoint, the dream world is a private world of the dreamer. Dream experiences are as real as waking experiences so long as the dream lasts; only on awaking does a man know that he was dreaming, because he realizes that his body and sense-organs were inactive in sleep. The subject and the object in the dream, and their relationship, are all created by atman from impressions received in the waking state and are illumined by the light of atman. The world of waking and the world of dreaming are both maya, because they project a manifold universe. Just as a fish swims between the two banks of a river without touching either of them, so atman wanders between the states of waking and dreaming unaffected by the experiences it encounters in either of these states. It is untouched by whatever it experiences, for "this infinite being is unattached."

When the dreamer passes into dreamless sleep, he is not aware of either the subject or the object, or of any specific consciousness. Vedanta says that in deep sleep there is a kind of union between the individual soul and the supreme soul. This union is merely apparent because the sleeper, on returning to the consciousness of the waking world, becomes his old self. In dreamless sleep atman remains covered by a thin layer of the veiling-power of maya, which fact accounts for its seeming unconsciousness. The experience of deep sleep gives a glimpse of the experience of Brahman, for in both states a man is free from fear, desire, and evil. In deep sleep, as in communion with Brahman, he knows nothing at all of the inner or outer world. "In this state a father is no father, a mother no mother, the worlds are no worlds, the Vedas no Vedas. In this state a thief is no thief, the killer of a noble brahmin is no killer. . . . [This form of his] is untouched by good works and untouched by evil works." In deep sleep consciousness is not really destroyed; there exists then an undifferentiated consciousness. The consciousness belonging to atman can never be absent, because it is imperishable by nature. If there were a real break in consciousness during deep sleep, one would then not recall, on awaking, any past experiences. Furthermore, should consciousness ever be broken, another consciousness would have to be postulated as the witness of this break. It appears, therefore, that in the relative world the nearest approach to the peace and desirelessness of Brahman, and also to the contentless consciousness felt in samadhi, or profound meditation, is the experience of deep sleep.

Atman in its purest form, detached from the three states and subsisting alone and by itself is, as already stated, called turiya; it is the same as pure consciousness or the unconditioned Brahman. It is non-dual and therefore free from good and evil. Though non-recognition of duality is common to both deep sleep and turiya, yet in deep sleep one knows nothing of either the self or the non-self, truth or untruth, while turiya is omniscient and all-seeing. Furthermore, in deep sleep relative experiences remain in seed forms ready to sprout again in the dream and waking states, whereas in turiya these seeds are roasted, as it were, in the fire of knowledge and cannot be brought back to life. Free from the notion of the empirical subject and object, turiya pervades all the phenomena of the relative universe, as the desert pervades a mirage. It is the unrelated ground of the three states, and is realized by the illumined soul as the unchanging non-dual reality.

As Hinduism admits the reality of the jiva or the embodied individual in the relative state, it also accepts the fact of its birth and death. What happens to the soul after death? The doctrine of absolute annihilation did not appeal to the Hindu mind, since it is inconsistent with the self-love innate in every normal person, and also because, in the eyes of Hinduism, it is in conflict with the moral order of the universe. In one brief crowded life it is impossible for a man to experience the fruition of all his actions, good and evil.

On the other hand, the doctrine of eternal happiness in heaven or eternal suffering in hell did not impress the philoso-

phers of the Upanishads. Happiness in heaven, being an effect,
cannot be eternal. Anything that has a beginning must also
have an end. Again, the theory of everlasting suffering is inconsistent with belief in God's love for created beings. The
soul, being an "eternal portion" of God, cannot be damned
forever. Furthermore, this theory reveals a total disproportion
between cause and effect: life on earth is exposed to errors and
temptations over which an individual cannot always exercise
control. To believe in the eternal punishment of the soul for
the mistakes of a few years, without giving it a chance for
correction, is to go against all the dictates of reason. Finally,
the destruction of the soul at death is inconsistent with the direct and intuitive experience of enlightened seers, who perceive
in deep meditation that the soul can exist independent of the
body.

Hinduism holds that after death the soul assumes a new
body and that this rebirth is governed by the law of karma. It
makes the claim that the soul's exit from the body, and its experiences after death, can be actually witnessed by the illumined person. They cannot, however, be demonstrated by
reason; furthermore, conditions being completely different on
the other side of the grave, the living would not understand
any report given by the dead. The doctrine of rebirth, based
upon the law of cause and effect, is the most plausible of all
the speculations regarding what happens to the soul after
death. It is an indispensable corollary of the immortality of
the soul, for without it a beginning of the soul would have to
be assumed. Thus the doctrine of rebirth is more probable than
improbable. One can live by it as if it were true. It explains
many phenomena of life which otherwise cannot be understood. What does he know of life who only one life knows?

The embodied soul instinctively feels itself to be limited and
bound by the finite body and seeks its freedom. It is bound by

desires, which create new births; but freedom comes from desirelessness. This desirelessness cannot be attained without experiencing the futility of all worldly desires. Desires are of
many kinds: some can be fulfilled in a human body, some in
a subhuman body, and others in a superhuman body. Thus a
soul experiences the fulfilment of desires through all kinds of
bodies ranging from the body of a blade of grass to that of the
highest deity in the phenomenal world. When it has fulfilled
every desire through repeated lives, without deriving any abid-
ing satisfaction, and finds the relative world to be bound by
the law of cause and effect, it longs for communion with Brahman, its real nature, which alone is untouched by the causal
law. The phenomenal universe being by its very nature limited, a Hindu seeking liberation does not want rebirth, be it
here on earth or in heaven. Liberation, in the Hindu tradition,
is liberation from repeated births and deaths.

All men are born with a blueprint of character, mainly pre-
pared by their actions in previous lives, though their physical
traits are determined by heredity. Men's present dispositions
are the results of their past, and their present actions create
their future. What is called fate or destiny is nothing but the
accumulation of tendencies created by past actions and
thoughts. Though it appears to be inexorable, fate can be
altered by new actions and thoughts of a contrary nature. A
man is the architect of his own fate, the builder of his own
destiny. Accepting with calmness his present experience, he
can by right conduct build up a happy future. If present suffering is the result of sinful actions in the past, then, in order
to avoid suffering in a future existence, a thoughtful man
should desire to sin no more. A man is not, however, altogether
a victim of the law of karma, or cause and effect; his real soul,
being divine, is free and unceasingly urges him to realize his
freedom. As through his good karma the veil of his ignorance

becomes thinner, he perceives more and more the divine nature of his soul and practises disciplines for its realization.

Hindu philosophers recognize three kinds of actions. Among
these, the most powerful action performed by a man in his
previous birth is responsible for his present body, which will
last as long as the momentum of the action lasts and will be
the medium for his pleasant and painful experiences. Illumined souls, whose minds are absorbed in the bliss of God, are
not disturbed by them, though the body and the organs may
be affected. There is a second kind of past actions, those which
will bear fruit in a future life. The third kind of actions, those
performed after the attainment of self-knowledge, bear no result, because the doer is entirely free from motive. This is explained by the illustration of the hunter. A hunter carries in
his hands a bow and an arrow, and on his back a quiver full of
arrows. He discharges the arrow at what he thinks to be a deer,
and not wanting to leave anything to chance, is about to shoot
a second one, when he discovers, to his dismay, that his target
was a man. In his revulsion he may now throw away the second arrow and also the quiver, but he cannot take back the
arrow which has left the bow. The arrow which has left the
bow represents the action which has determined a man's present body; the second arrow, about to be shot, the action performed after the attainment of knowledge; and the arrows in
the quiver, the past actions which have not yet begun to bear
fruit.

Not only the nature of our present life but also its duration
is determined by the actions and the unfulfilled desires of the
previous life. The body is the instrument through which desires
are fulfilled and serves no purpose after their fulfilment. This
accounts for the death of persons at different ages.

Death is one of the series of changes through which the
phenomenal soul passes: "Even as the embodied soul passes in

this body through the stages of childhood, youth, and old age, so does it pass into another body. Calm souls are not bewildered by this." "Even as a person casts off worn-out clothes and puts on others that are new, so the embodied soul casts off worn-out bodies and enters into others that are new." The Upanishad gives a vivid description of death and rebirth:

When the soul departs from the body, the life-breath follows: when the life-breath departs, all the organs follow. Then the soul becomes endowed with particularized consciousness and goes to the body which is related to that consciousness. It is followed by its knowledge, works, and past experience. Just as a leech supported on a straw goes to the end of it, takes hold of another support, and contracts itself, so does the self throw this body away and make it unconscious, take hold of another support, and contract itself. Just as a goldsmith takes a small quantity of gold and fashions another—a newer and better—form, so does the soul throw this body away, or make it unconscious, and make another—a newer and better—form suited to the Manes, or the celestial minstrels, or the gods, or Virat, or Hiranyagarbha, or other beings. . . . As it does and acts, so it becomes; by doing good it becomes good, and by doing evil it becomes evil—it becomes virtuous through good acts and vicious through evil acts.

A soul is born again and again, high or low, depending upon the merit or the demerit of its actions. The Upanishads speak of three courses which departed souls may follow before they are reborn on earth in a human body; it is through a human body that liberation is generally attained. Those who have led a life of extreme wickedness are born as subhuman beings. Those again who have discharged their social and moral duties, cherished desires, and sought the results of actions, repair after death to a heaven called the Plane of the Moon and reap there the fruit of their works, before they are reborn in a human body. But Brahmaloka, the highest heaven, is attained by those who have led an intense spiritual life on earth and sought the reality of God but failed in their effort. Some of the dwellers in Brahmaloka obtain liberation, and some return to earth. Such is the merry-go-round existence one leads in this phenomenal universe.

Man's eternal soul can never be permanently satisfied with non-eternal happiness. There is no real joy in the finite; real joy is only in the infinite. One who is tired of endless birth and death and heavy-laden with the experiences of the phenomenal world, which ultimately bring nothing but weariness, looks for the real freedom and bliss dwelling in every heart, but obscured by the veil of ignorance. Even the worst sinner—the vilest among men—at some time or other gets a glimpse of his real nature and becomes eager to realize it. He then practises spiritual disciplines in order to rid his mind of its impurities. The prodigal son turns his face to his Father's house.

Having dealt with adhyaropa, the superimposition of the unreal upon the real, we shall now discuss apavada, the refutation or negation of the unreal in order to realize the real. Through this process of negation one ultimately realizes that the world of unreal phenomena, superimposed upon reality by ignorance, is nothing but Brahman, just as the snake perceived in a rope is, in truth, nothing but the rope. It is not the reality of the universe that is negated, for that reality, being Brahman, always exists. What is negated is the illusory notion of the ignorant that the universe of name and form is real in itself, independent of Brahman. The description of the phenomenal world as maya, or illusion, is only a part of the Vedantic truth, the whole truth being that all that exists is Brahman. The knower of Brahman does not perceive any reality other than Brahman. Even while witnessing the creation, preservation, and destruction of the universe, he really sees that there exists Brahman alone, one and without a second.

The phenomenal universe is not the creation of an external agent, because the idea of an extra-cosmic Creator God is not accepted by Vedanta. Nor is the universe the modification of a cause. The modification is a mere name. There is no real difference between clay and its modification, a jar, except in the name and form. When the name and form are negated the jar is found to be nothing but clay. Thus, through the process of negation, the gross physical universe is discovered to be nothing but its cause, namely, the five gross elements, which, again, are found to be nothing but their cause, the five subtle elements. In this manner the subtle elements are found to be the same as their cause, the conditioned Brahman, who in turn is realized as the transcendental Brahman or pure consciousness. This Brahman is the uncaused great cause, the divine ground of everything that is perceived, and is identical with all.

The knowledge that the self is one with Brahman is liberation. Liberation is not the effect of knowledge, but knowledge itself. The relationship of cause and effect cannot be associated with the self, which is one and without a second. Furthermore, if liberation were the result of knowledge, it would have a beginning and an end, for whatever has a beginning also has an end. The self is always free, though this freedom can be concealed by maya, as the light of the sun by a patch of cloud. When the cloud is blown away, the sun's light becomes revealed; likewise, when maya is destroyed, the freedom of the self becomes manifest. Maya cannot destroy the self's freedom because freedom is its very stuff. If its freedom were destroyed, then the self would cease to be the self, as the sun would cease to be the sun if its light were destroyed.

The embodiment of the self is apparent and not real. Therefore its birth and death are also apparent only. A man endowed with knowledge of the self, though experiencing disease, old age, and death, remains unruffled by them because he knows that they are characteristic of the body and not of the self. He is also free from desire, which arises when one is identified with the body. For if a person has realized himself to be Brahman, infinite and all-pervading, and if he sees himself in the universe and the universe in himself, he cannot desire anything. What can he desire who has found the fulfilment of all desires in the self? The knowledge that the self is the desireless Brahman is liberation.

This is the Vedantic conception of immortality, an immortality not to be attained in heaven, but here on earth in this very body through the knowledge of the immortal nature of the self. About the enlightened person the Upanishads say: "Having always been free, he realizes his freedom." "If a person is able to attain knowledge in this very life, then this knowledge is real for him; if he does not attain knowledge in this very life, then a great destruction awaits him."

A knower of atman is called a jivanmukta; he is free while living in a physical body. How does a free soul act? How does he move? How does he behave?

A free soul is like a person who, having been sick, is made whole again; he is like one who, having been blind, has regained his sight; he is like one who, having been asleep, has again awakened. The attainment of self-knowledge is not a static condition beyond which the soul cannot move. This knowledge really indicates the soul's entrance into a new realm of consciousness. By his life and action, a free soul demonstrates the reality of Brahman, the divinity of man, and the oneness of existence.

Whether he is absorbed in meditation or conscious of the outer world, the illumination of a free soul is steady and his bliss constant. Though often he behaves like an ordinary person in respect to hunger and thirst, he is never oblivious of his true spiritual nature. Though active, he is not bound by the results of his actions, because he knows that the soul is neither the doer nor the enjoyer of the fruits of action; the spirit within him is always at peace. Free from worry, he does not dwell on the past, takes no thought for the future, and is unconcerned about the present. Death has no terror for him, being a mere change of body like a change of garments; he is the embodiment of fearlessness. Having realized the oneness of existence, he regards the pleasure and pain of others as his own pleasure and pain; he has not the slightest trace of selfishness.

Though a free soul lives in a world of duality, yet he remains undisturbed by its pairs of opposites. He may be tormented by the wicked or honoured by the good, but he is always unruffled. External happenings cannot produce any change in his soul, any more than rivers flowing into the ocean can disturb its bottomless depths. Even under repeated blows from the world he remains unshaken, like an anvil.

A free soul is bound neither by the injunctions of the scriptures, nor by the conventions of society, nor by the imperatives of ethics. Yet he cannot do anything that is not good or not conducive to the welfare of others, because long before his attaining the knowledge of Brahman, when he was still a seeker, he had suppressed all selfish desires and wicked propensities. Now he is free but not whimsical, spontaneous but not given to license. Though totally free in his action and thought, he never sets a bad example to others. The great ethical virtues, such as humility, unselfishness, sympathy, and kindness, which, prior to enlightenment, he assiduously cultivated for the purification of his mind, now adorn him like so many jewels. He does not seek them; they cling to him. Seeing himself in all beings, and all beings in himself, he is free from all unethical traits such as falsehood, greed, anger, and lust.

The greatness of a free soul can be known only by another

free soul. As a fish swimming in the water leaves no mark behind, or as a bird flying in the air leaves no footprints, so a free soul moves in the world unnoticed by others. A free soul is not a miracle-monger, nor does he advertise his holiness. But the ineffable peace radiating from his face bespeaks his holy nature. In his presence turbulent minds become quiet.

To ordinary men in society the free soul is an enigma. "Sometimes like a fool, sometimes like a sage, sometimes possessed of regal splendour, sometimes wandering about, sometimes behaving like a motionless python, sometimes wearing a benign expression, sometimes honoured, sometimes insulted, sometimes completely ignored—thus lives a free soul, ever happy in the knowledge of Brahman." Though without riches, yet he is ever content; though helpless, yet endowed with exceeding power; though detached from sense-objects, yet eternally satisfied; though outwardly active, yet inwardly actionless; though apparently enjoying the fruits of action, yet untouched by them; though dwelling in a finite body, yet he is ever conscious of his infinite nature.

A free soul no longer thinks in terms of bondage and liberation, which are concepts of the impure mind but never belong to atman, the spirit ever free. The embodied soul, on account of ignorance, becomes entangled in the relative life and then strives for liberation; but the enlightened soul sees neither birth nor death, neither bondage nor liberation.

A free soul, while living in the body, may experience disease, old age, or decay; may feel hunger, thirst, grief, or fear; may be a victim of blindness, deafness, or other deformities; but having realized that these are the characteristics of the body, the mind, or the senses, he does not take them seriously and so is not overwhelmed by them. A man who sees a play on the stage does not consider it to be real, yet he enjoys it to his heart's content; likewise, a free soul living in the midst of *reborn again + again until you are free from all desire(s)*

the joys and sorrows of the world enjoys them as the unfolding of a divine play.

A free soul lives, thinks, and works under the spell of immortality. And when his days on earth are completed, he departs from the world as if he were going from one room to another.

What happens to a knower of the self after death? Where does his soul go? The unillumined go to the upper or the nether world, or return to earth for the satisfaction of unfulfilled desires; but he who is desireless is not embodied again. "Of him who is without desires, who is free from desires, the objects of whose desires have been attained, and to whom all objects of desire are but the self—the life-breath does not depart. Being Brahman, he merges in Brahman." "When all the desires that dwell in his heart are gone, then he, having been mortal, becomes immortal and attains Brahman in this very body." Where could the omnipresent soul of the knower of atman go? Just as the lifeless slough of a snake is cast off and lies on an ant-hill, so does his body lie; his soul shines as Brahman. As milk poured into milk becomes one with the milk, as water poured into water becomes one with the water, as oil poured into oil becomes one with the oil, so the illumined soul absorbed in Brahman becomes one with Brahman. A free soul, however, out of compassion for mankind, may of his own free will again assume a human body and work for the welfare of mankind.

Once his ignorance is destroyed, a man enters into the realm of light, freedom, knowledge, and reality and never comes back to the world of darkness, bondage, ignorance, and illusion. Once the butterfly has emerged from the chrysalis, it no more crawls on the earth, but flits from flower to flower, bathed in the light of the sun.

Such is the ultimate destiny of the human soul.

IV.

Hindu Ethics

ETHICS, which concerns itself with the study of conduct, is derived, in Hinduism, from certain spiritual concepts; it forms the steel-frame foundation of the spiritual life. Though right conduct is generally considered to belong to legalistic ethics, it has a spiritual value as well. Hindu ethics differs from modern scientific ethics, which is largely influenced by biology; for according to this latter, whatever is conducive to the continuous survival of a particular individual or species is good for it. It also differs from utilitarian ethics, whose purpose is to secure the maximum utility for a society by eliminating friction and guaranteeing for its members a harmonious existence. Hindu ethics prescribes the disciplines for a spiritual life, which are to be observed consciously or unconsciously as long as a man lives.

Hindu ethics is mainly subjective or personal, its purpose being to eliminate such mental impurities as greed and egotism, for the ultimate attainment of the highest good. Why Hindu ethics stresses the subjective or personal value of action will be discussed later. Objective ethics, which deals with social welfare, has also been considered by Hindu thinkers. It is based upon the Hindu conception of dharma, or duty, related to a man's position in society and his stage in life. Objective ethics, according to the Hindu view, is a means to an end, its

57

purpose being to help the members of society to rid themselves of self-centredness, cruelty, greed, and other vices, and thus to create an environment helpful to the pursuit of the highest good, which transcends society. Hinduism further speaks of certain universal ethical principles which apply to all human beings irrespective of their position in society or stage in life.

The ethical doctrines of the Hindus are based upon the teachings of the Upanishads and of certain secondary scriptures, which derive their authority from the Vedas. But though their emphasis is mainly subjective, the Upanishads do not deny the value of social ethics. For instance, we read: "As the scent is wafted afar from a tree laden with flowers, so also is wafted afar the scent of a good deed." Among the social virtues are included "hospitality, courtesy, and duties to wife, children, and grandchildren." In one of the Upanishads, a king, in answer to a question by a rishi regarding the state of affairs in his country, says: "In my kingdom there is no thief, no miser, no drunkard, no man without an altar in his home, no ignorant person, no adulterer, much less an adulteress."

Ethical action calculated to promote social welfare is enjoined upon all who are identified with the world and conscious of their social responsibilities. Without ethical restraint there follows social chaos, which is detrimental to the development of spiritual virtues. According to the Upanishads, the gods, who are the custodians of society, place obstacles in the path of those who seek liberation from samsara, or the relative world, without previously discharging their social duties. As a person realizes the unreality of the world and the psycho-physical entity called the individual, his social duties gradually fall away; but they must not be forcibly given up. If the scab is removed before the wound is healed, a new sore forms. Every normal person endowed with social consciousness has a threefold debt to discharge: his debts to the gods, to the rishis, and to the ancestors. The debt to the gods, who favour us with rain, sun, wind, and other natural amenities, is paid through worship and prayer. The debt to the rishis, from whom we inherit our spiritual culture, is paid through regular study of the scriptures. The debt to the ancestors, from whom we have received our physical bodies, is paid through the propagation of children, ensuring the preservation of the line. With the blessings of the gods, the rishis, and the ancestors, one can cheerfully practise spiritual disciplines for the realization of the highest good, in which all worldly values find fulfilment. The observance of social ethics, in a large measure, preserved Hindu society when various outside forces threatened to destroy it. The neglect of social ethics, on the other hand, has undermined its vitality.

How, by suitable ethical disciplines, the brutish man may become a decent man, the decent man an aristocrat, and the aristocrat a spiritual person, has been explained by a story in one of the Upanishads. Once a god, a man, and a demon—the three offspring of the Creator—sought his advice for self-improvement. To them the Creator said: "Da." As the syllable *da* is the first letter of three Sanskrit words, meaning, respectively, self-control, charity, and compassion, the Creator was in effect asking the god to practise self-control, the man charity, and the demon compassion. In human society there exist aristocrats, average men, and demoniacal men. The aristocrat, in spite of his education, refinement, generosity, and gentleness, may lack in self-control and go to excess in certain matters like eating, drinking, or gambling. Hence he needs self-control to improve his character further. The average man, in spite of his many human qualities, is often greedy; he wants to take what belongs to others. Liberality or charity is his discipline for self-improvement. The demoniacal person takes delight in treating others with cruelty and ruthlessness, which can be suppressed through the practice of compassion. The Upanishads say that the Creator, even today, gives the same moral advice to different types of human beings through the voice of the thunderclap, which makes the reverberating sound "Da-da-da."

The caste system in Hinduism is intimately connected with the social aspect of Hindu ethics, demonstrating the importance of renunciation and self-denial as cardinal virtues. The origin of this system is found in the Vedas, though it later underwent much transformation in the hands of the Hindu law-givers. The Bhagavad Gita says that the Lord Himself divided human beings into four groups, determined by their actions and virtues. Traditions other than Hinduism support similar divisions. Plato divided the state into three classes, castes, or professions, namely, philosopher-rulers, warriors, and the masses. Nietzsche says that every healthy society contains three mutually conditioning types and that it is nature, not Manu, the Hindu law-giver, which separates one from another: the mainly intellectual, those mainly endowed with muscular and temperamental strength, and those who are distinguished neither for the one nor for the other, the mediocre third class. The first group contains select individuals, and the last, the great majority.

According to the Hindu scriptures, a normal society consists of the brahmins, who are men of knowledge, of science, literature, thought, and learning; the kshatriyas, who are men of action and valour; the vaisyas, who are men of desires, possessiveness, and acquisitive enterprise; and lastly the sudras, who are men of little intelligence, who cannot be educated beyond certain low limits, who are incapable of dealing with abstract ideas, and who are fit only for manual labour. Each of them, in the words of Nietzsche, has its own hygiene, its own domain of labour, its own sentiment of perfection, and its own special superiority. In the Vedas the four castes are described as four important parts of the body of the Cosmic Person: the head, the arms, the thighs, and the feet. This analogy suggests the interdependence of the four castes for the common welfare of all; it also suggests that the exploitation of one by another undermines the strength of the whole of society. The rules regarding the four castes sum up the experience, sagacity, and experimental morals of long centuries of Hindu thinkers.

The Bhagavad Gita describes the virtues of the four castes, and their duties. The qualities of a brahmin are control of the mind and the senses, austerity, cleanliness, forbearance, uprightness, scholarship, insight, and faith. He possesses a minimum of worldly assets, accepts voluntary poverty, and is satisfied with simple living and high thinking. Both a priest and a teacher, he is the leader of society and an adviser to king and commoner. A custodian of the culture of the race, he occupies his high position in society by virtue of his spirituality, and not by the power of arms or wealth. The qualities of a kshatriya are heroism, high spirit, firmness, resourcefulness, dauntlessness in battle, generosity, and sovereignty. Agriculture, cattle-rearing, and trade are the duties of a vaisya. The main duty of a sudra is action entailing physical labour.

The hierarchy in the caste system is determined by the degree of voluntary renunciation, poverty, and self-control, and also by the degree of intellectual and spiritual attainments. A brahmin has to suppress many impulses for physical enjoyment. A kshatriya, no doubt, enjoys power and pleasure, but he is ready at any time to lay down his life for the protection of the country from external aggression or internal chaos. A vaisya, whose moral code and intellectual attainments are not so rigorous or high as those of the two upper castes, amasses wealth, both for his own enjoyment and for the welfare of society. One does not expect from a sudra very much of spiritual, intellectual, or moral perfection. The higher is one's position in the caste system, the greater is one's obligation to members of the lower castes, and the more stern is the renunciation of personal comforts. *Noblesse oblige.* The caste system was designed to promote the harmonious working of society, the weak being assured of protection from the strong. "It is a law of spiritual economics," said Mahatma Gandhi; "it has nothing to do with superiority or inferiority." When a person belonging to a lower caste becomes a saint, he is honoured even by the brahmins. The disciplines for spiritual development are not withheld from anyone.

The basis of the caste system, according to the Hindu view, is men's self-evident inborn inequality: physical, intellectual, and spiritual. An individual is born into a higher or lower caste as a result of actions performed by him in his previous life, and each person, therefore, is himself responsible for his position. By discharging the duties determined by his caste, a man becomes qualified for birth in a higher caste in a future life. If one does not accept the doctrine of rebirth and the law of karma, then the inequity from which members of lower castes often suffer cannot be explained.

A second element in the organization of the caste system is varna or colour. Even in the remote past of history, the Indian subcontinent was inhabited by people of different racial groups marked by different complexions, which formed the basis of their divisions. In course of time, through trade relations and invasions, the Persians, the Greeks, the Scythians, the Bactrians, the Sakas, the Kusanas, the Huns, and peoples of other races entered India and were gradually absorbed into Hindu society. They were assigned places in the caste system according to their physical or mental aptitudes. In this manner Hindu society solved the problem of alien minorities in its midst. Gradually the contrast between colours was toned down by intermarriages. Through permutations and combinations many subcastes came into existence. A tolerant Hindu society allowed the newcomers to preserve, as far as practicable, their own racial preferences regarding food, clothes, and social and religious customs. This perhaps explains the existence of a great diversity in India in regard to these matters. A composite Hindu society gradually came into being, whose watchwords were unity in diversity and friendly coexistence. In olden times inter-dining was permitted, as also intermarriage under certain conditions. Through the caste system, Hindu society entrusted itself to the leadership of spirituality and intellect in preference to that of military power, wealth, or labour.

As the population increased and other complexities set in, the qualities of the individual became less easy to determine and heredity was gradually accepted as a sort of working principle to determine the caste. The son inherited the professional duties of the father as well as some of his physical and mental traits. But in olden times, when a brahmin did not live up to his virtues, he was demoted, and a sudra, by the acquisition of higher qualities, was promoted. Conduct was more important than birth. One of the Upanishads narrates the touching story of Satyakama, a young boy who wanted to study the Vedas, a privilege accorded only to one who was born in the brahmin caste. When the boy asked his mother about his lineage, she said that she did not know it because she had conceived him when, as a young woman, she had been preoccupied with many household duties and had had no time to ask his father about his lineage. When the teacher whom Satyakama approached for the Vedic knowledge heard this he was impressed

with the boy's truthfulness and outspoken nature and con-
cluded that his father must have been a brahmin.

For many centuries the caste system worked in a superb
manner, creating and consolidating the Indian culture, which
reached its height when the brahmins, kshatriyas, vaisyas, and
sudras all dedicated their activities and efforts to the common
welfare. But in this relative universe even a good custom, if
it continues for a long time, becomes corrupted. The brahmins
had a monopoly of the knowledge of the scriptures, which was
the source of their power; eventually they became greedy for
more and began to exploit the lower castes. They demanded
privileges and respect even when they did not possess brah-
minical qualities. Similarly, the kshatriyas and the vaisyas exploited the sudras, who formed the majority of the population.
The social laws became rigid, and in the absence of freedom
Hindu society stagnated. On account of exploitation, the
masses became weak and the country fell an easy prey to
powerful invaders from the outside. Islam and Christianity
took advantage of the injustices that prevailed in Hindu society and made easy converts, especially among those who
were denied social privileges. Hindu society, however, was not
completely to blame; for these foreign religions also sometimes
used force and unethical persuasion for the purpose of con-
version.

But it should not be forgotten that the caste system, even in
its rigid form, rendered good service to Hindu society during
the days of foreign domination. The brahmin leaders, by
means of iron-clad caste laws, prevented Islam and Christianity from completely destroying it. They became the custodians
of the Hindu culture and zealously protected it from the level-
ling influence of these alien faiths.

Contact with the West revealed to the Hindu leaders many
drawbacks in their society and made them aware of the need

for drastic changes in the caste system. Since India's attainment of political freedom, laws are being enacted for the gradual elimination of taboos about marriage, inter-dining, and social intercourse. The lower castes are being given greater facilities for education, and no one is being debarred from government jobs on account of his caste. It is to be hoped that this unique social system, which has in the past decisively contributed to India's spiritual life, will again create an environment in which men and women will be able to practise the virtues stressed in Hinduism for the realization of the final goal of human evolution.

The Bhagavad Gita states, in its last verse, that the secret of prosperity, strength, morality, and all-round social welfare lies in the harmonious working together of the spiritual and the royal power. Sankaracharya points out that a conflict between the brahmins, the creators of the spiritual culture, and the kshatriyas, the protectors of that culture, causes the disintegration of society. If India gives up the caste system in principle and in practice, she will surely lose her spiritual backbone. There is, however, no room for the caste system in an industrialized society, which is controlled largely by the power of wealth and labour. It is the goal of a secular classless society to create an equality on the level of the sudras, whereas Indian society, through the caste system, has aimed at creating an equality by raising all to the level of the brahmins.

Even at its best, however, the caste system is a human institution, and one cannot expect perfection of it. The good and evil of the rule of society by the four castes have been brilliantly pointed out by Swami Vivekananda in a letter to an American friend written during the last decade of the nineteenth century. The Swami says:

Human society is, in turn, governed by the four castes—the priests, the soldiers, the traders, and the labourers. Each state has its glories as well as defects. When the priest (brahmin) rules, there is a tremendous exclusiveness on hereditary grounds—the persons of the priests and their descendants are hemmed in with all sorts of safeguards—none but they have any knowledge. Its glory is that at this period is laid the foundation of the sciences. The priests cultivate the mind, for through the mind they govern.

The military (kshatriya) rule is tyrannical and cruel; but they are not exclusive, and during that period the arts and social culture attain their height.

The commercial (vaisya) rule comes next. It is awful in its silent crushing and blood-sucking power. Its advantage is that, as the trader himself goes everywhere, he is a good disseminator of the ideas collected during the two previous states. They are still less exclusive than the military, but culture begins to decay.

Last will come the labour (sudra) rule. Its advantages will be the distribution of physical comforts—its disadvantages (perhaps) the lowering of culture. There will be a great distribution of ordinary education, but extraordinary geniuses will be less and less.

If it is possible to form a state in which the knowledge of the priest period, the culture of the military, the distributive spirit of the commercial, and the ideal of equality of the last can all be kept intact, minus their evils, it will be an ideal state. But is it possible?

Yet, the first three have had their day, now is the time for the last—they must have it—none can resist it. . . . The other systems have been tried and found wanting. Let this one be tried— if for nothing else, for the novelty of the thing. A redistribution of pain and pleasure is better than always the same persons having pains and pleasures. The sum total of good and evil in the world remains ever the same. The yoke will be lifted from shoulder to shoulder by new systems, that is all.

Let every dog have his day in this miserable world, so that after this experience of so-called happiness they may all come to the Lord and give up this vanity of a world and governments and all other botherations,

Outside the pale of society are the untouchables, whose contact pollutes others. Who are these untouchables? Originally they were the aborigines, with a very low mental development, who ate unclean food, lived by hunting, and were uncouth in appearance, manner, and conduct. The Aryans, proud of their spiritual culture, shrank from them. But instead of annihilating them outright, or forcibly superimposing upon them their own higher culture, the Aryans sought to assimilate them through education. The *Ramayana* and the *Mahabharata* record that many of these aborigines established intimate friendships with the Hindus of the higher castes. During the foreign rule of India, when the very existence of Hinduism was threatened, society became conservative and the process of assimilation practically stopped. Now that the danger is over, laws have been passed abolishing untouchability. Economic and political positions, educational facilities, and temple entry for the purpose of worship are open to all. Even in the past many Hindu religious leaders have protested against untouchability and regarded it as a blot upon society.

Apart from caste, a person's duties, in the Hindu tradition, are determined by the stage of life to which he belongs. Life, which is regarded by Hinduism as a journey to the shrine of truth, is marked by four stages, each of which has its responsibilities and obligations. In that journey a normal person should leave no legitimate aspiration unfulfilled; otherwise physical and mental sickness will follow, putting roadblocks in the way of his further spiritual progress.

The first stage of life covers the period of study, when a student cultivates his mind and prepares himself for future service to society. He lives with his teacher in a forest retreat and regards the latter as his spiritual father. He leads an austere life and conserves his energy, spurning the defilement of the body and mind through evil words, thoughts, or deeds.

He shows respect to his elders and teachers, and becomes acquainted with the cultural achievements of the race. Students, rich and poor, live under the same roof and receive the same attention from the teacher and his wife. When the studies are completed, the teacher gives the pupil the following instruction, as described in one of the Upanishads:

Speak the truth. Practice dharma. Do not neglect the study [of the Vedas]. Having brought to the teacher the gift desired by him, [enter the householder's life and see that] the line of progeny is not cut off. Do not swerve from the truth. Do not swerve from dharma. Do not neglect [personal] welfare. Do not neglect prosperity. Do not neglect the study and teaching of the Vedas. Do not neglect your duties to the gods and the Manes. Treat your mother as God. Treat your father as God. Treat your teacher as God. Treat your guest as God. Whatever deeds are faultless, these are to be performed—not others. Whatever good works have been performed by us, those should be performed by you— not others. Those brahmins who are superior to us—you should comfort them by giving them seats. Now, if there arises in your mind any doubt concerning any act, or any doubt concerning conduct, you should conduct yourself in such matters as brahmins would conduct themselves—brahmins who are competent to judge, who [of their own accord] are devoted [to good deeds] and are not urged [to their performance] by others, and who are not too severe, but are lovers of dharma. Now, with regard to persons spoken against, you should conduct yourself in such a way as brahmins would conduct themselves—brahmins who are competent to judge, who [of their own accord] are devoted [to good deeds] and are not urged to their performance by others, and who are not too severe, but are lovers of dharma. This is the rule. This is the teaching. This is the secret wisdom of the Vedas. This is the command [of God]. This you should observe. This alone should be observed.

With marriage, a person enters the second stage. A normal

person requires a mate; his biological and emotional urges in this respect are legitimate. Debarred from marriage are those alone who have a dangerous ailment that may be transmitted to children, or those rare souls who, as students, forsake the world at the call of the spirit. Neither a confession of sin nor a concession to weakness, marriage is a discipline for participation in the larger life of society. Children endow marriage with social responsibilities; Hinduism does not regard romance as the whole of the married life. Husband and wife are co-partners in their spiritual progress, and the family provides a training ground for the practice of unselfishness. A healthy householder is the foundation of a good society, discharging his duties as a teacher, a soldier, a statesman, a merchant, a scientist, or a manual worker. He should be ambitious to acquire wealth and enjoy pleasures, but not by deviating from the path of righteousness. The following are the five great duties of a householder: the study and teaching of the Vedas; daily worship of the gods through appropriate rituals; gratification of the departed ancestors by offering their spirits food and drink according to the scriptural injunctions; kindness to domestic animals; and hospitality to guests, the homeless, and the destitute.

When the skin wrinkles, the hairs turn grey, or a grandchild is born, one is ready for the third stage of life in the forest or in a quiet place. At this stage, the pleasures and excitements of youth appear stale and physical needs are reduced to a minimum. The third period of life is devoted to scriptural study and meditation on God.

During the fourth stage, a man renounces the world and embraces the monastic life. He is no longer bound by social laws. The call of the infinite becomes irresistible to him; even charity and social service appear inadequate. He rises above worldly attachments, finite obligations, and restricted loyalties;

he is a friend of his fellow human beings, of the gods, and of
the animals. No longer tempted by riches, honour, or power,
a monk preserves equanimity of spirit under all conditions. He
turns away from the vanities of the world, devoting himself to
the cultivation of God-consciousness, which is a man's true
friend both here and hereafter. During the fourth stage, a dis-
ciplined life attains to its full blossoming. Well has it been
said: "When a man is born he cries and the world laughs; but
let him lead such a life that when he dies, he laughs and the
world cries."

Thus it will be seen that every stage of life, as described in
the Vedas, has its duties and obligations, the right discharge of
which requires self-control. Through the disciplines of the four
stages of life, a Hindu learns progressive non-attachment to the
transitory world. The movement of life has been aptly compared to that of the sun. At dawn the sun rises from below the
horizon, and as the morning progresses it goes on radiating
heat and light till it reaches the zenith at midday. During the
afternoon it goes down, gradually withdrawing its heat and
light, and at dusk it sinks below the horizon, a mass of radi-
ance, to illumine other regions.

The key to the individual and social ethics of Hinduism is
the conception of dharma, whose full implications cannot be
conveyed by such English words as religion, duty, or righteousness. Derived from a root which means *to support,* the word
signifies the law of inner growth by which a person is supported in his present state of evolution and is shown the way
to future development. A person's dharma is not imposed by
society or decreed by an arbitrary God, but is something with
which he is born as a result of his actions in previous lives.
Dharma determines a man's proper attitude toward the outer
world and governs his mental and physical reactions in a given
situation. It is his code of honour.

Hinduism emphasizes the relative nature of dharma, and does not recognize absolute good or evil; evil may be described as what is less good. One cannot stipulate what is absolutely good or evil for all men at all times. The attempt to do so, and to judge all people by a single concept of dharma or impose upon all a single idea of righteousness, has been the cause of much injustice to humanity. If one wants to give a comprehensive definition of good and evil, one may say that what helps men toward the realization of God or of the unity of existence is good, and its reverse is evil. But one faces difficulties when one tries to work out practical details. A soldier unsheathes his sword to vindicate law and justice, whereas a saint lays down his own life for the same purpose. The injunction of non-killing cannot therefore have a universal application, at least at the present state of human evolution. A man must not give up his imperfect dharma, determined by his inborn nature; all actions have elements of imperfection in them. He should follow his own dharma and should not try to imitate the dharma of another, however perfect the latter may be. By performing his duties in a spirit of worship without seeking any personal result, a man ultimately realizes God, in whom alone all duties and values of life find their fulfilment. The *Mahabharata* narrates the stories of a housewife and an untouchable butcher who, by following their respective dharmas, realized the highest truth and became teachers of the knowledge of Brahman.

The affirmative attitude of Hinduism toward life has been emphasized by its recognition of four legitimate and basic desires: dharma or righteousness, artha or wealth, kama or sense pleasure, and moksha or freedom through communion with God or the Infinite. Of these, the first three belong to the realm of worldly values; the fourth is called the supreme value. The fulfilment of the first three paves the way for moksha.

Enjoyment, if properly guided, can be transformed into spiritual experience. The suppression of legitimate desires often leads to an unhealthy state of body and mind, and delays the attainment of liberation.

Dharma, or righteousness, we have already seen to be the basis of both individual progress and social welfare. Artha, or wealth, is legitimate; money is indispensable in the present state of society. Voluntary poverty, as practised by religious mendicants, is something quite different; pious householders provide for the monks' few necessities in recognition of their efforts to keep alive the highest spiritual ideal. But a man of the world without money is a failure; he cannot keep body and soul together. According to an injunction of Hinduism, first comes the body and next the practice of religion. Furthermore, money is needed to build hospitals, laboratories, schools, museums, and educational institutions, which distinguish a civilized from a primitive society. Money gives leisure, which is an important factor in the creation of culture. But money must be earned according to dharma; otherwise it debases a man by making him greedy and cruel.

The object of the third legitimate desire is kama, or the enjoyment of sense pleasure. This covers a vast area—from the enjoyment of conjugal love, without which the creation cannot be maintained, to the appreciation of art, music, or poetry. Life becomes drab and grey unless one cultivates aesthetic sensitivity. But sense pleasures, if not pursued according to dharma, degenerate into sensuality. Wealth and sense pleasure, which are only means to an end, are valuable in so far as their enjoyment creates a genuine yearning for spiritual freedom in the mind of the enjoyer. The hedonists alone regard sense pleasure as an end in itself.

The Charvaka school of thinkers, out-and-out materialists, rejects righteousness and spiritual freedom and admits only two values, namely, those related to wealth and sense pleasure. The Upanishads make a sharp distinction between the ideal of the pleasant and of the good, and declares that the former, created by ignorance, ultimately brings about suffering and misery. Even dharma, or duty, for its own sake, is regarded as empty and dry by Hindu philosophers. It is a worthy end in so far as it helps the soul to attain its spiritual goal. But the illumined person serves the world not from a sense of duty but because of his overflowing love for all created beings.

The fourth legitimate desire, equally irresistible, is related to moksha, or freedom from the love and attachment prompted by the finite view of life. Man, who in essence is spirit, cannot be permanently satisfied with worldly experiences. The enjoyment of desires reveals the fact that desires cannot be satisfied by enjoyment, any more than fire can be quenched by pouring butter into it; the more they are fulfilled, the more they flare up. Nor can man attain his divine stature through correct social behaviour, economic security, political success, or artistic creation. Charity for the needy may be a corrective for selfishness, but cannot be the ultimate goal of his soul's craving. Even patriotism is not enough: as history shows, undue emphasis on patriotism was a major cause of the downfall of the Greek city-states. After fulfilling all his worldly desires and responsibilities a man still wants to know how he can suppress his inner restlessness and attain peace. So at last he gives up attachment to the world and seeks freedom through the knowledge of the spirit.

A few words may be said here to explain why Hindu philosophers emphasized personal ethics over social ethics. Their argument was that since society consisted of individuals, if individuals were virtuous, social welfare would follow as a matter of course. Second, the general moral tone was very high in the ancient Hindu society, where everybody was expected to do his appropriate duties, which included, among other things, rendering help to one's less fortunate fellow beings. As the country was prosperous and men were generous and hospitable, no need was felt for organized charity, which, even in Europe and America, has been a comparatively new development. The organized social service in the modern West is, to a large extent, a form of sentimentalism in reaction against the doctrine of utilitarianism and the industrialization of Western society due to the extraordinary growth of science and technology. Third, the Hindus regarded spiritual help as of more enduring value than material help: the hungry would feel again the pinch of hunger, and the sick would again be sick; but a spiritual person could easily bear with calmness his physical pain and privations. Finally, Hindu philosophers believed that the sum total of physical happiness and suffering remains constant. Suffering, like chronic rheumatism, only moves from one place to another but cannot be totally eradicated. It is not easy to substantiate the claim of progress, if it means the gradual elimination of evil and increase of good. It is true that we are living in a changing world, but it need not be true that we are living in a progressive world. Every age has its virtues and limitations; but can anyone really show that men today are enjoying more happiness, peace, and freedom than their forebears? The Hindu philosophers, without encouraging the illusion that a perfect society could be created, always exhorted people to promote social welfare as a part of spiritual discipline. We must do good to others, because by means of selfless action we can purify our hearts and transcend the relative world of good and evil. Social service has only an instrumental, not an ultimate, value.

But the need for emphasis on social ethics in modern India cannot be denied. For times have changed; the conception of dharma, which was the foundation of Hindu life, both individual and social, has greatly lost its hold upon the people. The struggle for existence in an increasingly competitive society has become keen, and wealth is not justly distributed. The strong often invoke the law of karma to justify their exploitation of the poor, who are helpless in their suffering. There exists in India a widespread misery due to ignorance, poverty, ill health, and general backwardness. The rich and the powerful are often too selfish to remove these drawbacks. Hinduism in the past has no doubt produced many saints; but the precious gems of their spiritual realizations have been preserved in heaps of dirt and filth.

A certain measure of compliance with the general principles of social ethics may well have helped to preserve the Hindu social system from total disintegration during the dark period of Indian history. But on account of insufficient emphasis on social responsibilities, there is in Hindu society a lack of the vitality characteristic of Western society. Therefore India is now emphasizing the value of social ethics; the government is trying to create a welfare state. Whatever may be the pattern of development in the new India, she should not forget the ultimate goal of ethics, namely, the liberation of the soul from the bondage of the phenomenal world.

From what has been said above it will be clear that social ethics is efficacious in so far as it helps a person to curb his selfishness. But Hindu philosophers have recognized that social duty also has its limitations. Duty is often irritating; behind it is the idea of compulsion and necessity. Thus a person constantly engaged in the discharge of his duty finds no time for prayer, meditation, study, recreation, or other things which his soul craves. If the kingdom of heaven is within a man, he cannot attain it by always looking frantically outside. It is often under the guise of duty that a man indulges his greed, passion, desire for domination, or morbid attachment. When stretched too far duty becomes a disease. As Vivekananda has said: "Duty is the midday sun which scorches the tender plant of spirituality."

Hindu philosophers encourage the performance of duties, but they exhort men to perform them not from a sense of compulsion but through love. Unless a man is inspired by love, he cannot cheerfully perform his duty at home, in the office, in the factory, or on the battlefield. This love is not, however, sentimentality, but springs from the perception of God in all living beings. Work done under the impulsion of duty deepens a man's attachment to the world, but when performed through love it brings him nearer to freedom.

The healthy social environment created by objective ethics provides men with an opportunity to cultivate the more important subjective ethics. The disciplines of subjective ethics for the liberation of the soul have been stressed in the Bhagavad Gita and the Upanishads. The Gita says: "Let a man lift himself up by his own self; let him not depress himself; for he himself is his friend and he himself is his enemy. To him who has conquered himself by himself, his own self is a friend, but to him who has not conquered himself, his own self is hostile like an external enemy."

The chief disciplines of subjective ethics are austerity, self-control, renunciation, non-attachment, and concentration. Austerity enables a man to curb his impulses for inordinate enjoyment of physical comforts and also for the acquisition of supernatural powers which exalt him far above the world of men, nay, even above the world of the gods. In the Upanishads austerity, or tapas, often denotes intense thinking, the same sort of thinking which precedes creative work, making a man indifferent about his personal comforts or discomforts. But later austerity degenerated into bodily torture as practised by spurious yogis with a view to performing miracles for selfish purposes, thus depriving this noble virtue of its original significance.

Let us try to understand the meaning of self-control. The sense-organs, which are ordinarily inclined toward material objects and employed to seek only the pleasant, should be controlled in order to create that inner calmness without which profound spiritual truths cannot be grasped. But self-control does not mean the weakening of the organs, as is explained in the Katha Upanishad by the illustration of the chariot. The body is compared to the chariot, the embodied soul to its master, the intellect or discriminative faculty to the driver, the mind to the reins, the senses to the horses, and sense-objects to the roads. The chariot can serve its purpose of taking the master to his destination if it is well built, if the driver can discriminate between the right and the wrong road, if the reins are strong, if the horses are firmly controlled, and if the roads are well chosen. Likewise, the spiritual seeker should possess a healthy body and vigorous organs, unerring discrimination, and a strong mind. His discrimination should guide his senses to choose only those objects which are helpful to the realization of his spiritual ideal. If the body, the mind, or any of his faculties is injured or weakened, he cannot attain the goal, just as the rider cannot reach his destination if the chariot and its accessories are not in the right condition. Thus the two important elements emphasized in the practice of self-control are discrimination and will-power. The middle path, which makes a man "temperate in his food and recreation, temperate in his exertion in work, temperate in sleep and waking," has been extolled by the Bhagavad Gita and also by Buddha.

Renunciation is another discipline for self-perfection. A good example of it is seen in the institution of monasticism. A monk takes the vow of renouncing enjoyments in the "three

worlds"—earth, the mid-region, and heaven. The four stages
of life, already described, are a training ground for this important discipline. Non-attachment and concentration will be
discussed in a later chapter.

Ethics is principally concerned with conduct, which is in
turn guided by will, pious or impious. The impious will leads
to unrighteous conduct and produces evil, whereas the pious
will leads to righteous conduct and is conducive to the highest
good. With the help of ethical disciplines one suppresses unrighteousness and stimulates righteousness.

Unrighteousness may be physical, verbal, or mental. Physical unrighteousness is expressed through cruelty, theft, and
sexual perversion; verbal unrighteousness through falsehood,
rudeness, insinuation, and gossip; mental unrighteousness
through ill-will, covetousness, and irreverence.

Righteousness is also threefold: physical, verbal, and mental. Physical righteousness is expressed through charity, succour to the distressed, and service to all; verbal righteousness
through gentle speech conducive to the welfare of others; and
mental righteousness through kindness, detachment, and reverence. Righteousness and unrighteousness cover both personal
and social duties. Broadly speaking, virtue is defined as what
is conducive to the welfare of others, and vice as what causes
them pain and misery.

Patanjali, in his yoga philosophy, enumerates the important
virtues as follows: non-injury, truthfulness, abstention from
theft, chastity, and non-attachment to material objects. Non-
injury and truthfulness are sovereign virtues emphasized by
all religious Hindus, from the Vedic seers to Mahatma Gandhi.
The practice of non-injury also includes gentleness and abstention from harsh words. Mahatma Gandhi applied non-
injury as a discipline for the individual and for the nation.

Chiefly by means of non-violence, India, under his leadership, secured her political freedom from alien rule.

Truthfulness implies the ascertainment of facts by such valid proofs as direct perception, correct inference, and reliable testimony. In addition, truthfulness demands that facts must be described without any intentional deceit or unnecessary verbiage. Such truthfulness is often lacking in diplomatic statements and political discussions. Half-truths and evasions are regarded as lies. But truthfulness, in order to be effective, must not unnecessarily hurt the feelings of others, its purpose being the welfare of others. When such a purpose is not served the wise remain silent. A Hindu injunction says: "Speak the truth; speak the pleasant, but not the unpleasant truth."

Abstention from theft requires not only that one should not appropriate another's property unlawfully but also that one should abstain from greediness. What it really amounts to is indifference to the material advantages of life. The accumulation of physical objects beyond a certain limit is generally tainted by cruelty, greed, or similar blemishes. One cannot hoard wealth without some sort of deceit or injury to others.

The practice of chastity, highly extolled by Hindu philosophers, includes abstention from lewdness in thought, speech, and action. According to a strict definition, as applied to monks, a man becomes unchaste not merely through the sexual act, but even when he listens to or utters lewd words, engages in a sport or looks at an object which arouses lust, exchanges secrets with a member of the opposite sex, or expresses the desire or makes the effort for carnal gratification. Both the body and the heart must be kept unsullied by a spiritual seeker, the body being the temple of God and the heart its inner shrine.

The Bhagavad Gita speaks of the spiritual virtues as the "divine treasures" with which an aspirant provides himself in his search for God. Their opposites—for instance, ostentation, arrogance, self-deceit, anger, rudeness, and ignorance—belong to those who are born to the heritage of the demons. Here is a graphic description from the Gita of men of demoniac nature:

They do not know what to do and what to refrain from. Purity is not in them, nor good conduct, nor truth. They say: "The world is devoid of truth, without a moral basis, and without a God. It is brought about by the union of male and female, and lust alone is its cause—what else?" Holding such a view, these lost souls, of little understanding and fierce deeds, rise as the enemies of the world for its destruction. Giving themselves up to insatiable desires, full of hypocrisy, pride, and arrogance, they hold false views through delusion and act with impure resolve. Beset with innumerable cares, which will end only with death, looking on the gratification of desire as their highest goal, and feeling sure that this is all; bound by a hundred ties of hope, given up wholly to lust and wrath, they strive by unjust means to amass wealth for satisfaction of their passions. [They say to themselves:] "This desire I have gained today, and that longing I will fulfil. This wealth is mine, and that also shall be mine. That enemy I have slain, and others, too, I will slay. I am the lord of all, I enjoy; I am prosperous, mighty, and happy. I am rich; I am of high birth. Who else is equal to me? I will offer sacrifice, I will give, I will rejoice." Thus deluded by ignorance, bewildered by many fancies, addicted to the gratification of lust, they fall to the lowest depths of degradation.

According to the Bhagavad Gita, the "three gateways of hell" leading to the ruin of the soul are lust, wrath, and greed, and the five cardinal virtues are purity, self-control, detachment, truth, and non-violence. Called universal virtues, they admit of no exceptions arising from caste, profession, place, or occasion. They are compulsory for all spiritual seekers aspiring after freedom, and they differ from ordinary moral standards, by which one treats differently men and animals, one's fellow countrymen and foreigners, relatives and strangers.

Jainism, which is an offshoot of Hinduism, speaks of an action as immoral if it is impelled by the impious thought of the agent, and moral if there is pious thought behind it. Forgiveness is regarded as the highest virtue. Jaina ethics aims more at self-culture than at social service, though in actual practice the Jainas of India are most forward in alleviating miseries, especially those of dumb animals and insects.

Buddhist philosophers hold that it is not words or tangible actions alone that are moral or immoral, but also the disposition of the mind. Thus unrighteousness begins to accumulate from the day when a man resolves to earn his living by plundering and killing others, though the resolution itself may remain unfulfilled for a long time. Likewise, a man begins to accumulate virtue from the day he makes a pious resolution, even though the conscious action may take place much later. Furthermore, Buddhism admits of institutional morality: the founder of an institution is responsible for its good and bad effects upon others. Thus the founder of an alms-house engages in a meritorious action, whereas the founder of a temple where animals are slaughtered is guilty of an immoral act.

Greek ethics stresses the social virtues, the two most prominent ones being justice and friendship. Of these, the former emphasizes proper respect for the rights of others, and the latter is a social quality.

Many thinkers, both Eastern and Western, find it difficult to reconcile ethics with non-dualism. It is argued that ethical laws can have meaning only in a world of duality, and non-dualism denies the reality of such a world. This contention is based upon a misconception of non-dualism. It is true that from the absolute standpoint Brahman alone is real and the universe and individual souls, as such, are unreal. But from the relative standpoint neither the physical universe nor individual souls can be repudiated, nor birth and death, pain and pleasure, good and evil, virtue and vice, and the other pairs of opposites. As long as a person sees imperfection, he cannot remain indifferent to ethical virtues; but when everything appears as Brahman, no question of ethics arises. Admitting the empirical reality of the phenomenal universe, the non-dualistic Vedanta has formulated its ethics, cosmology, theology, and philosophy with a view to enabling the embodied soul to realize its oneness with Brahman.

The non-dualistic ethics can be regarded from two standpoints: ascetic or negative, and affirmative. Let us first consider the ascetic aspect. Under the influence of nescience or ignorance there appears an individual soul who regards the world of diversity as real. First he forgets the non-dual nature of his soul, and next entertains the wrong belief that he is separate from others. He sees a physical and social environment to which he reacts in diverse ways: he develops love or hate for certain individuals, and remains indifferent toward the rest. Thus it is not merely forgetfulness of one's true nature but also the perception of other individuals as separate from oneself which is the cause of suffering. The idea of ego, which arises when the soul through ignorance identifies itself with the body and senses, is the source of all evil; selfishness is sin. Hence a man seeking freedom and peace should give up identification with the body and the sense-organs, and all private and personal attachments. Therefore non-dualistic ethics, in one of its phases, preaches the ascetic or the negative discipline of the suppression of ego.

Now let us consider the affirmative aspect of the non-dualistic ethics. Man is more than the narrow and finite self; he is Brahman, the All, and it is his duty to recognize his oneness with all. But a theoretical recognition is not enough; his daily action must demonstrate it. A man trying to understand the nature of his relationship with others should be told that all individuals, being of the nature of the spirit, are in essence identical with one another. Consequently it is his duty to avoid discrimination between one being and another, and cultivate a feeling of kindliness and love for all. For the non-dualist this love is not confined to men, but extends to all living creatures. Love for one's neighbour means love for every living being, and this all-embracing love is based upon the fact that all living beings have souls, though all souls may not have reached the same state of spiritual growth. The universal love taught by non-dualism is based upon the realization of the fundamental oneness of all living beings. The apparent difference between one being and another is entirely due to ignorance; the wise see the same spirit everywhere. Even the exclusive love shown by the ignorant is an expression of the universal love based upon the non-duality of the spirit. Whether one knows it or not, the oneness of existence is the only source of mutual attraction. The husband loves the wife not for the sake of the wife but for the sake of the spirit which dwells in both.

Now, the question arises whether a man, still cultivating ethical disciplines, can transcend the strife and contradictions which are the characteristics of the phenomenal world, and experience the peace and freedom which his higher nature seeks. Is ethics an end in itself, or does it lead to a higher state in which all ethical laws are transcended?

Hindu philosophers believe that no real freedom or peace is possible as long as a man is identified with the domain of ethical laws. Moral life cannot be dissociated from struggle—an incessant struggle against the evil and imperfection which seem to be always present on the relative plane. Ethics is concerned with life as it *ought* to be lived. A moral man constantly says to himself: "I ought to have done this, I ought not have done that." Therefore *oughtness* is the very crux of morality and implies an unceasing struggle for self-improvement. Moral life belongs to the plane of imperfection. No one can be *merely* moral and at the same time perfect; for oughtness and imperfection go together. Where there is no imperfection there is no *ought;* the *ought* itself implies imperfection.

The struggle against evil cannot be won on the moral level; for morality cannot redeem the sinner. The woman taken in adultery, as described in the Bible, was condemned by her judges according to the moral laws of the time, but could not be redeemed by them. The redemption came from a spiritual man, *der reine Tor,* who had transcended moral laws and was the embodiment of innocence and guilelessness. How could the moral judges, themselves still struggling against evil, enable the woman to rid herself of her sin? One is redeemed through love and grace, which belong to the realm of spirit. Dirt cannot be completely washed away by water which is less dirty, but only by water which has no trace of dirt.

Hindu philosophers have suggested the means of enjoying spiritual freedom even while engaging in the performance of action. Both optional duties, through which the agent seeks particular ends, and obligatory duties, which ought to be done by all spiritual seekers endowed with social consciousness, should be performed according to the moral laws. But the actions of the enlightened, performed in a spirit of love and non-attachment, cannot bind the doer; the secret of freedom is non-attachment. This non-attachment is not a negative attitude; it is not indifference. On the contrary, it denotes a superior power of the mind which enables one to preserve inner peace and equanimity in success and failure. The practice of non-attachment by both the dualist and the non-dualist will be discussed in the chapter dealing with karma-yoga.

Both enlightened dualists and non-dualists, free from ego, transcend the moral *ought*. In their activity they are not impelled by the compulsion of duty, but by love. Action flows spontaneously from the fullness of their hearts. To them the idea of work with the purpose of improving the world is meaningless. Devotees of God see the world as God's world, His playground, and regard themselves as His playmates. Non-dualists see everywhere and in everything only the spirit, ever perfect, ever free, and ever illumined. The world-process is the spontaneous manifestation of the spirit, as the waves are of the ocean, there being neither rhyme nor reason behind the cosmic activity. To project, support, and dissolve names and forms is the very nature of Brahman, say the Upanishads. Only the ignorant read a motive into the creation. Their little brains fool them all the time.

Work of lasting benefit to humanity has been done by blessed souls like Christ and Buddha, who were free from ego and the moral struggle, and inspired by selfless love for all. On the other hand, the work done by many social reformers or philanthropists has a limited value. It is said that nowadays men become philanthropists only after making their first million; even in a noble act of charity there is a conscious or unconscious desire for fame, power, or recognition. Too often a philanthropist is trying to soothe a guilty conscience or escape the boredom of life. And how different modern charity is from the charity of St. Francis, inspired by his love, humility, chastity, poverty, and complete self-denial. Only an illumined person, whose ego has either been burnt in the fire of self-knowledge or totally transformed by love of God, has no trace of selfish motive. Sankaracharya says that a man should first of all see God in himself, and then serve others as manifestations of God. Such a man alone can perform really unselfish and therefore fruitful action. His moral struggles are over. He is no longer deceived by the notion of good and evil. He does not refrain from evil from fear of punishment or engage in good works from hope of reward; moral virtues become his natural attributes, the by-products of his spiritual freedom. In the words of the Upanishad: "Evil does not overtake him, but he transcends evil. He becomes sinless, taintless, free from doubts, and a knower of truth."

V.

work, action

Spiritual Disciplines I (Karma-Yoga)

"IN THAT which is night to all beings," says the Bhagavad Gita, "men of self-control are awake; and where all beings are awake, there is night for the contemplative who see." The meaning of this passage is that to the unenlightened the supreme reality is like night; while trying to understand it they see darkness and confusion. But the enlightened are fully awake with regard to reality. Further, the physical world of names and forms is clear as day to the unenlightened, but the enlightened see in it the darkness of night. An Upanishad says: "The self-willed Supreme Lord inflicted an injury upon the sense-organs in creating them with outgoing tendencies; therefore with them a man perceives only outer objects, and not the inner self. But a calm person, wishing for immortality, beholds the inner self with eyes closed." The worldly man directs his sense-organs to the enjoyment of physical objects; but a spiritual seeker, by means of spiritual disciplines, turns his organs toward the inner self.

The mind is by nature pure and clear, and capable of reflecting reality. The impurities in it, which distort the image of reality, are created by desires and attachments. Being foreign to it, they may be removed; and this is effected through the practice of spiritual disciplines. Thus the unenlightened man becomes enlightened.

It is direct perception that gives an object the stamp of reality. God and the soul, which form the very basis of religion, appear unreal or vague to the unenlightened because neither of them is directly perceived, whereas physical objects appear real and clear because they are directly perceived. It is a commonly accepted view that direct knowledge is obtained through the senses, and indirect knowledge through the testimony of another—a man or a book. A person may sometimes have an intellectual idea of God or the soul, yet they are not vital to him because they are not proved by direct knowledge. There is, however, a possibility of deception in many so-called direct perceptions by the sense-organs. A mirage is perceived by the eye and yet it is not real. Any abnormal physical condition can distort a man's view of external objects; for instance, a rise in the bodily temperature may conjure up many unreal visions which appear to be directly perceived. Be that as it may, direct knowledge cannot be repudiated by indirect knowledge. The apparent reality of the physical world cannot be negated by the mere testimony of the scriptures or the mystics, but only by the direct experience of another kind of reality, which Vedanta calls Brahman. This direct experience can be obtained by spiritual disciplines, which in Hinduism are called yoga. Christ said: "Seek and you will find; knock and it will open." Here he referred to spiritual disciplines and direct experience.

The real meaning of the scriptures becomes revealed to one who has practised spiritual disciplines. The scriptures of the different religions cannot be reconciled if one emphasizes only the letter and overlooks the spirit. For instance, Christianity, on the basis of the Bible, believes in the Trinity and regards Christ as the only begotten son of God. Islam, on the basis of the Koran, strongly upholds the unity of God and denies that He can ever beget a son. But it is often forgotten that the scriptures can only indicate the supramental reality, and never directly describe its true nature. According to the Vedas, a knower of Brahman transcends the scriptures. The prophets use inadequate human speech to describe what is beyond mind and speech; they also shape their teachings to suit the requirements of the place, time, and the understanding of their devotees. Therefore in order to understand the real meaning of the scriptures or the teachings of the prophets, one must acquire inner experience through the practice of spiritual disciplines. If the prophets of different religions were to meet, they would certainly say that they were proclaiming the same truths; but the gibberish and the grimaces of their fanatical followers never come to an end.

The Hindu philosopher, unlike Plato, is not content with a merely intellectual understanding of reality; for such an understanding is not of much value in times of practical need. Reality must be directly known, and the knowledge of reality should then be applied in daily life. The Sanskrit word for philosophy is *darsana*, which means *seeing*, and not mere love of knowledge. What is the use of philosophy if it does not enable a man to commune with reality? And has one who communes with reality any further need of philosophy? The ultimate goal is direct communion with the spirit, and this communion is made possible through spiritual discipline.

In the Bhagavad Gita, Arjuna asks Krishna: "Under what compulsion does a man commit sin, in spite of himself, and driven, as it were, by force?" Krishna replies: "It is desire, it is wrath, which springs from rajas.[1] Know that this is our enemy here, all-devouring and the cause of all sin." The direct manifestation of rajas is the insatiable fire of desire which envelops knowledge and is the foe of wisdom. Under the pressure of rajas, a man harbours greed, lust, and anger. Rajas

[1] See pp. 27–28.

attacks a person through the senses, the mind, and the understanding, veiling knowledge and deluding the embodied soul.
Stern spiritual disciplines are necessary to control rajas.

As has been stated before, in Hinduism the general name
for spiritual disciplines is yoga, which means, literally, union
of the individual self with the supreme self, and also the
method of this union. There are different kinds of yoga suited
to different temperaments. The kind of yoga that is applicable
to a man is determined by his innate tendencies. Though there
are as many minds as there are human beings, yet the Hindu
psychologists speak of four general types: active, emotional,
introspective, and philosophical; and for each there is an appropriate yoga. It is true that each mind contains some of the
four traits, but one particular trait is dominant and this dominant trait indicates the type of the spiritual discipline a person
should pursue.

Work when performed as a spiritual discipline is called
karma-yoga. It is the predominant topic of the Bhagavad Gita,
though the book deals with other yogas as well. The purpose
of the teachings of the Bhagavad Gita is to solve a moral
problem. Krishna, an avatara, was the teacher, and Arjuna,
a warrior, the disciple. There was a bitter quarrel between
two royal families of cousins. The family to which Arjuna
belonged was the more righteous. Truth and justice were at
stake, and Arjuna was determined to defend them. At first
Krishna and the other wise men tried their utmost to make
a peaceful settlement, but on account of the intransigeance of
the other family, they failed. War became inevitable. Among
the combatants on both sides Arjuna found brothers, uncles,
teachers, sons, nephews, and friends—to whom he was bound
by a thousand ties of love, respect, and affection. Clearly fore-
seeing that the destruction accompanying the war would be
followed by family disintegration and social chaos, he was re-

luctant to accept the responsibility, and said to Krishna that he would like to retire from the battlefield, go into a forest, and lead the life of a religious mendicant. Confused, he asked Krishna to show him the path of duty.

Arjuna's dilemma was caused by his confusion about the two ideals which, from time out of mind, have moulded the Hindu pattern of life. These are the disciplines of action and renunciation, distinctly laid down for two types of mind. The discipline of action is followed by the majority of men, who believe in social obligations and who do not explain away the world and the individual ego as unreal. They seek happiness here and hereafter. But a few persons who realize self-knowledge to be the supreme duty of life and who are convinced of the transitory nature of all material experiences either on earth or in heaven follow the discipline of renunciation, and seek liberation from bondage to the phenomenal world. Both disciplines are necessary to preserve the social stability; but their spheres must not be confused. Arjuna obviously was not ready for the discipline of renunciation because he was conscious of his duty to society and was still attached to his relatives and friends, whose death he anticipated with sorrow. Certainly he had not attained that spiritual elevation from which one sees the illusory nature of worldly values, good or evil. He talked about renunciation only as an escape from the unpleasant duties of life. Krishna characterized this attitude as "lowness of spirit, unbecoming a noble mind, dishonourable, and detrimental to the attainment of heaven, which every warrior covets." He advised Arjuna to plunge into action and fight in a spirit of non-attachment: "He who sees non-action in action, and action in non-action, he is wise among men, he is a yogi, and he is the doer of all actions." "He who is free from the notion of egotism, and whose understanding is undefiled—though he slays these men, he really slays them not

nor is he stained by the result of slaying." This non-attachment
is the secret of work as a spiritual discipline.

Mere karma or action is different from karma-yoga, or action as a spiritual discipline. Karma is what is done, a deed.
Activity is seen everywhere, both in physical nature and in
man. Nature is active; for one sees activity in the stars and
the planets, trees and rocks; space itself is vibrating. And there
is something in the very make-up of man—the spirit of rajas
—which drives him to action in spite of himself. His body is
active when he is awake; his mind is active, both in the waking and dream states; and his heart, lungs, and other organs
are always active, even in deep sleep. The body cannot be kept
alive if one remains inactive. The preservation of the social
order, too, demands constant and vigilant action. Even religious disciplines, such as prayer, worship, and meditation,
are forms of activity. Though actionlessness may characterize
a certain form of spiritual experience, it cannot be attained
without previous practice of the discipline of action.

By means of action, according to Hindu philosophers, one
promotes a harmonious relationship between men, the deities,
and subhuman beings, and thus keeps the "wheel of creation"
moving. All created beings are interdependent and sustain
one another by their actions. Thus action has a cosmic significance. He who ignores the cosmic significance of action and
works only for his selfish purpose lives in vain. "He who cooks
only for himself eats sin." According to the Bhagavad Gita,
when the Lord, in the beginning, created men, He planted in
them a propensity for action and gave the mandate that they
should not only multiply by work but also thereby fulfil their
desires for happiness.

When work is done without any desire for personal gain it
becomes spiritual action. Such work is utterly different from
the mechanical action seen in the inorganic world, or the in-

stinctive action at the infra-rational level, or the egocentric action of an average person.

Ordinary karma has a binding quality. It creates and leaves behind subtle impressions, which at a future time and under favourable conditions become the causes of new actions. The new actions likewise create another set of impressions which in their turn become the causes of yet other actions. So man works impelled by necessity; he has no freedom. Now the question arises as to how one can avoid the bondage of the causal law and work as a free agent. The solution lies in karma-yoga. Karma-yoga is the secret of action. It gives the worker evenness of mind in gain and loss, success and failure.

How is one to acquire evenness of mind? There are two elements in all voluntary actions. First, there is the immediate feeling of pleasure or pain arising from the contact of the senses with their objects; and second, the longing for the result, which generally provides the incentive for action. The sensations of pleasure and pain, though inevitable, are impermanent; therefore calm souls endure them without becoming distracted. Even when sensations are pleasant one should not be attached to them, because after they disappear one misses them, and if they persist too long one feels bored. As regards the result, it should not be the incentive for action. The illumined person does not work for a result. "To the work alone," the Bhagavad Gita says, "you have the right, never to its fruit. Do not let the fruit of action be your motive; and do not be attached to non-action." This is the meaning of the statement that your left hand must not know what your right hand does. Every action, following the causal law, will surely produce its fruit; why long for it? "Wretched are they who work for results." If an action is done without attachment to its fruit, evenness of mind is sure to follow. Action should be *action should be* natural and spontaneous, prompted by the exigencies of a situation. When you see a needy person, you should spontaneously help him if you are capable, without taking into consideration what you may gain in return. A karma-yogi may even participate in a war to protect law and order, provided he is unselfish and free from greed or passion.

It is not renunciation of action itself, but renunciation of the longing for the fruit, that is the secret of karma-yoga. As long as a man remains conscious of his social obligations or sees wrong being done to others, he cannot remain inactive. It is true that at an advanced stage of spiritual progress one gives up all actions and remains absorbed in contemplation, thereby enjoying real peace. But mere abstention from action is not spiritual non-action, which is experienced when one forgets oneself in the contemplation of God. "He who restrains the organs of action but continues to dwell mentally on the objects of the senses deludes himself and is called a hypocrite." Therefore, for an active mind, it is positively harmful to renounce obligatory action on the false pretext of cultivating the attitude of non-action. Furthermore, the relinquishment of duty for fear of inflicting physical suffering upon oneself or others does not bring about the desired fruit of spiritual non-action. One must not shun a duty because it is disagreeable, nor become attached to it because it is agreeable. But if an active person cheerfully performs a duty because it is to be done, and renounces all attachment to its result, he obtains the fruit of renunciation, namely, inner peace.

Hinduism recommends total renunciation of the world for the attainment of the highest good. But true monastic life, however desirable, is not easy; genuine monks are few and far between, and false monks are a real nuisance to society. Therefore Hinduism asks average men to perform their duties as householders and at the same time preserve the spirit of re-

nunciation. What is needed is not renunciation *of* action, but
renunciation *in* action. The ordinary duties of life should not
be abhorred, but selfishness must be suppressed.

The eighteenth chapter of the Bhagavad Gita explains various factors of karma-yoga, such as knowledge, the doer, understanding, firmness, and happiness. The doer's knowledge,
without which he cannot perform any voluntary action, should
be characterized by an all-embracing sense of unity in the
midst of diversity. Likewise, the doer himself should be free
from attachment and egotism, endowed with fortitude and
zeal, and unruffled by success or failure. Right understanding
is that by which he can discriminate between good and evil,
bondage and liberation, work and rest. Right firmness is accompanied by unswerving concentration and control of the
mind and senses. Right happiness may be like "poison" at first
but is like "nectar" in the end; it is born of direct self-knowledge and acquired by steady practice. And lastly, action itself,
in order to have a spiritual meaning, should have a bearing
upon the social welfare and be performed without attachment
and aversion.

To summarize the secrets of karma-yoga: First, give up
brooding over the fruit of action. Brooding begets attachment;
attachment, the desire to possess; frustrated desire, anger;
anger, delusion; delusion, self-forgetfulness; and self-forgetfulness brings about ultimate destruction. Second, do not be a
beggar. Give all you can but never ask for the fruit. It is not
work that wears one out but constant thinking about its fruit.
Third, pay as much attention to the details of work as to its
ultimate goal. Once you have a mental picture of the glorious
goal you expect to attain, you may for the time being drop it
from your thought and be busy about the dreary details. Ideal-
ize the real, then you will realize the ideal. The real cause of
failure in our various undertakings is to be found most often

in our carelessness about the details. Fourth, one should remember that there is no such thing as a perfect action; every action contains an element of imperfection, just as fire contains smoke; the imperfect element of the action cannot affect the doer if he is totally unselfish. A judge, in condemning a criminal to death, does not incur sin.

From what has been said it will be noticed that one can practise karma-yoga without believing in a conventional religion or God, or adhering to any creed. Simply through unselfish action one can gradually attain to the state of inner peace and freedom which is reached by a religious devotee through love of God or by a mystic through contemplation. "Be good and do good" seems to be the essence of the teaching of Buddha, who cut himself away from the dogmas and creeds of the popular Hinduism of his time. But the goal is more easily reached by average persons if their actions are inspired by certain religious beliefs. Such beliefs make non-attachment easier to practise.

Broadly speaking there are two kinds of religion: one, the dualistic, associated with the Personal God, and the other, the non-dualistic, associated with impersonal reality, though it may be argued that the latter cannot properly be called religion. Dualists aim at God-realization mainly through love, and non-dualists at self-realization through philosophical discrimination. Action performed in the right spirit can help both dualistic and non-dualistic aspirants to realize their respective ideals.

Dualists should realize that God alone is the real doer, and that man is an instrument in His hand. They should work for God's satisfaction, and see God in all living beings. Service to men is a form of worship. A devotee of God feels blessed that God has chosen him as one of His instruments. To him success or failure is beside the point. He considers himself a sword in

God's hand, and lets God use him in any manner He likes. He feels a joy in being made, a joy in being used, a joy in being broken, and a joy in being finally thrown aside after his mission is fulfilled. As a result of selfless action, the devotee's heart is purified. It becomes free of ego, lust, and greed. The pure man sees in his own heart, and in the hearts of others as well, vivid reflections of God. "He treats all beings alike and attains supreme devotion to God." Infinite compassion flows from his universal heart. The Lord says in the Bhagavad Gita: "By devotion he knows Me, knows what in truth I am and who I am. Then, having known Me in truth, he forthwith enters into Me."

A follower of non-dualism, too, can attain self-realization through action. At the outset he should practise discrimination between the self and the non-self. He should realize that the self is the immortal spirit, the serene witness of the activities of the non-self, whereas the non-self, consisting of the body, sense-organs, mind, and ego is the doer, the instrument of action, and the enjoyer of the fruit. The self is the unchanging infinite, and the non-self the mutable finite. It is obvious that the self and the non-self, spirit and matter, are as different from each other as light and darkness. Yet on account of maya the self identifies itself with the non-self and regards itself as both the actor and the enjoyer of the fruit of action. Thus the pure and ever free self becomes a victim of the pleasure and pain of the phenomenal world. The goal of non-dualistic spiritual discipline is to separate the self from the non-self and to enable it to realize itself as the witness of the activities of the non-self.

A non-dualist practising karma-yoga should perform work in the light of discrimination between the self and the non-self. He should keep in mind that though a deluded person thinks he is the doer, it is really the non-self which is the agent, the instrument of action, and the enjoyer of the fruit. The sensations of pleasure and pain, through contact with agreeable and disagreeable objects, are natural for the senses. The wise man remains the witness of their appearance and disappearance without coming under their control. To him all actions are the "preoccupation of the senses with their objects," of nature with nature, of gunas with the gunas. The self or spirit, by its proximity, animates insentient nature and itself looks on as one unconcerned. It acts like a lamp, whose light enables a man to perform either a good or a bad deed and experience an appropriate result, while remaining itself the unconcerned witness. " 'I do nothing at all,' thinks the non-dualist, for in seeing, hearing, touching, smelling, and tasting; in walking, breathing, and sleeping; in speaking, emitting, and seizing; in opening and closing the eyes—he is assured that it is only the senses that are busied with their objects." Working without attachment, he remains "untouched by sin, as a lotus leaf by water." He thus dwells happily in the body, the "city of nine gates," neither working nor causing work to be done, though outwardly appearing to be active. He sees non-action in action. Even when the body and mind are intensely active, he sees the self as the actionless spirit immersed in peace; this is the real non-action of an illumined soul.

The result of such discipline is purity and serenity of mind. The man of pure mind engages in hearing about the self, reasoning about the self, and lastly, contemplating the self with unwavering devotion. In the depths of contemplation, he realizes his inner spirit as identical with the supreme spirit of the universe. He experiences the oneness of existence. "With the heart concentrated by yoga, viewing all things with equal regard, he beholds himself in all beings and all beings in himself."

The enlightened person sees God manifested both as the

One and as the many. He communes with the One in the silence of meditation, and with the many through work. Thus to him the farmyard, the laboratory, the battlefield, or the market is as proper a place for communion with God as the temple, the cloister, the mountain cave, or the monk's cell. But this lofty attitude cannot be maintained unless a person has become firmly rooted in the oneness of existence.

Karma-yoga can be an effective spiritual discipline for persons who seek knowledge of God or knowledge of the self. The result in either case is purification of the mind, followed by love of God or knowledge of the self. In the final stage all actions drop away, and the devotees are completely absorbed in their respective ideals. For a dualist there remains a slight distinction between himself and God, though the ordinary notion of ego associated with the idea of possessiveness has been transcended. In self-realization complete unity is experienced. Afterwards both the dualist and the non-dualist can resume their outer activities for the welfare of the world. Even then they practise daily communion with God or with the self. Christ, after his hard work of spiritual ministration during the day, retired in the evening from the multitude to commune with his Heavenly Father. As the lives of illumined souls have been completely transformed by the knowledge of truth, their actions are free from the slightest trace of selfishness. It is such actions that confer lasting blessings upon mankind.

VI.

Spiritual Disciplines II (Bhakti-Yoga)

Yoga of Divine Love

A MAN'S action may be compared to the flight of a bird, which needs three things—two wings and a tail—for its graceful movement. By means of the wings it balances itself in the air, and by the tail, like the rudder in a boat, it keeps its course. In a worker, love and knowledge are the two wings, and meditation the tail. When these function harmoniously, the action becomes graceful. Let us now discuss love as a spiritual discipline. This is called bhakti-yoga, or the yoga of divine love.

Love as a force of attraction operates at different levels: the material, the human, and the spiritual. On the material level it draws together the particles of an inanimate object; on the human level it joins friend and friend, parents and children, husband and wife; and on the spiritual level it unites a man with God. The real source of attraction is the spirit or God; a particle of matter cannot of itself attract another particle. Because God as spirit pervades the whole universe and because He is the inmost self of all beings, one sees the force of attraction operating everywhere. There is no essential difference between a lower form of attraction, for instance the attraction of a mistress for her lover, and a higher form of attraction, such as the attraction of children for the mother. The apparent difference is due to the difference in the channels through which the love is expressed.

Love is a creative force, and through creation one seeks joy and immortality. Desiring this joy some who are virile in body beget offspring, and some who are virile in mind create art, compose poetry, write philosophy, organize states, or engage in similar pursuits. There are yet others, virile in spirit, who through love beget God-consciousness, the bestower of the highest good. Through creation one hopes to become immortal. Parents expect immortality through their offspring, as the poet, the artist, the philosopher, the statesman, and the scientist through their respective work. The lover of God seeks everlasting life through union with Him.

A lover finds joy in beauty and shrinks from ugliness. Birds and animals choose spring for their mating season; human lovers seek beautiful surroundings; and lovers of God always search for beauty, which for them is the good. Love based upon physical attraction, called worldly love, is short-lived, unsatisfactory, and inadequate, because the objects of such love are material forms which are impermanent and limited. It is based upon such external factors as physical beauty, which is ephemeral, name and fame, wealth, power, and position, which too are transient. One is also afraid to offend one's beloved for fear of losing her love. Neither spontaneous nor natural, it harbours an element of jealousy. Furthermore, worldly love constantly changes. A baby is absorbed in his mother. When he grows up he becomes interested in his school-fellows. Then he marries and his wife fills up his heart. Next come children. Even the love of heaven, which is brightly painted by the popular religions, is a form of material love; the denizens of heaven, too, enjoy material objects. The difference between the enjoyments in heaven and on earth is not one of kind but merely one of degree; life in heaven is a continuation of earthly life. A worshipper of God is a materialist if he seeks physical enjoyment here and hereafter.

Love based upon intellectual attraction is more impersonal and enduring. Thus if friendship or conjugal love has for its support common philosophical, artistic, or other intellectual interests, it will last longer than love based upon physical factors, which contains the seeds of quick deterioration. It is a matter of common observation that the more intellectually developed the life of a person is, the less he takes pleasure in the objects of the senses. No man enjoys his food with as great satisfaction as a dog or a pig. The life of the animal lies entirely in its senses, which in many cases are keener than those of human beings. The primitive man obtains more happiness from physical objects than does an educated man; but he is denied the joy arising from the contemplation of music, philosophy, or science. The offspring of intellectual love is more satisfying than that of physical love. What earthly offspring can compare with the intellectual offspring left behind by Homer, Kalidasa, Beethoven, Asoka, or Leonardo da Vinci? The same is true of immortality; the immortality conferred by intellectual offspring is infinitely more enduring than that conferred by physical offspring. But intellectual immortality, too, is a relative one. The most satisfying love is associated with God; divine love is immortal because God is immortal. In it there is no trace of ugliness, because God is the source of pure beauty, whose reflection one sees in the beauty of the physical and intellectual creation. When love of God fills the heart all other forms of love pale into insignificance. One star rises, then comes a bigger one, and next a still bigger. As the bigger star appears, the smaller one becomes dim. At last the sun, the biggest star, appears, and all the others fade out. God is the biggest star, and the lover of God is not interested in worldly love, physical or intellectual. Although he does not, like an agnostic or an atheist, deny heaven, he is not interested in it, because it is inadequate to satisfy the yearning of his soul. The unceasing craving of his immortal spirit finds no satisfaction in any finite, perishable material object. The Katha Upanishad narrates the story of Nachiketa, who sought from his teacher the knowledge of the imperishable self. When tempted by the teacher with gold, cattle, children, grandchildren, and a long life on earth and in heaven, the pupil said: "But these will endure only till tomorrow. Furthermore, their enjoyment exhausts the vigour of the sense-organs. Even the longest life is short indeed. Keep your horses, dances, and songs for yourself." In the Brihadaranyaka Upanishad one reads the story of Maitreyi who was offered her share of property by Yajnavalkya, her husband and teacher, as he was about to embrace the monastic life. She said to him: "Venerable sir, if indeed the whole earth full of wealth belonged to me, would I be immortal through that or not?" "No," replied Yajnavalkya, "your life would be just like that of people who have plenty. Of immortality, however, there is no hope through wealth." Then Maitreyi said: "What should I do with that which would not make me immortal? Tell me, venerable sir, of that alone which you know to be the means of attaining immortality."

One cannot fully enjoy the love of God unless one rises above all worldly attractions. In the teachings of Christ one sees the utter incompatibility between the Kingdom of Heaven, which lies within a man's heart, and the kingdom of the physical world. But worldly love is not futile, because it is also the love of the spirit; though clogged and distorted with mortal matter, it provides the love-hungry soul with various steps by which love of God can finally be realized. Through these successive steps the possessive attraction is gradually transformed into self-negating divine love. The experience gained through the enjoyment of worldly love teaches a man about its impermanence. Then he feels the irresistible attraction of God,

who, like a huge magnet, is always drawing living creatures to
Him. On account of the mental impurities produced by attachment to the world, a man does not feel the force of this
attraction, as a needle coated with mud is not attracted by a
magnet. But when his mind becomes pure through the practice of detachment, he feels the attraction of God and longs to
be united with Him.

Spiritual love, or bhakti, is directed only to God, whose effulgence puts to shame "a million suns, a million moons, and
a million gods of beauty." He is the Personal God, or the spirit
in the form of a person. One of the bhakti scriptures says:
"The sages who are satisfied with the supreme self and who
are free from all the ties of the world, show to the Personal
God a love that knows no reason; such is the greatness of
God." "He, the Lord, is of His own nature ineffable love."

God, the object of the devotee's love, is sometimes described
as a projection of the human mind. Hinduism emphatically
repudiates this view. According to non-dualism, it is Brahman
which, through maya, its own inscrutable creative power, appears as God. If the form of God is a projection of the mind,
it is Brahman itself that projects this form for the purpose of
creating the universe and helping the devotees. Therefore,
from the non-dualistic viewpoint, the Personal God is as real
as the universe and living beings. When the universe and living beings ultimately merge in Brahman, God too becomes one
with it. According to the qualified non-dualist Ramanuja, the
ultimate reality is the Personal God, which is non-dual but admits of the distinction of inanimate nature and living beings,
both of which form part of Him. According to the dualist
Madhva, the Personal God, the universe, and living beings are
all real. To return to the non-dualistic position: the Personal
God is the highest manifestation of the Absolute in the relative

universe; as from the relative standpoint the creation is without beginning or end, so is He without beginning or end.

When a man obtains love of God, he loves all, hates none, and becomes satisfied for ever. It is that same intense love which non-discriminating persons have for the fleeting objects of the senses. When love of God is fully developed, the lover forgets both the world and the body, so dear to all. This love cannot be exploited for any worldly purpose—neither for health, nor for wealth, nor for longevity, nor for happiness in heaven. It cannot be genuine if the lover shows the slightest attachment to the world. In it there is no room for jealousy or hatred, because the devotee sees everything as the manifestation of God. Bhakti is both the ideal of spiritual life and the means to its attainment.

The discipline of bhakti is the easiest and most natural of all spiritual disciplines, because it does not demand the suppression of normal impulses; it only tells the devotee to turn them to God. Thus he is asked to feel passionate desire to commune with God, to feel angry with himself for not making spiritual progress, to feel greedy for more spiritual experiences, and so on. But without the most rigorous training, love of God may degenerate into dangerous emotionalism, one manifestation of which is bigotry. The narrow-minded worshipper often measures his devotion to his own religious ideal by the amount of dislike he shows for the religious ideals of others. In the history of religion nothing has been more directly responsible for cruelty, hatred, and bloodshed than fanaticism.

Ramanuja, a great teacher of bhakti-yoga, speaks of the preparations necessary for the development of genuine love of God:

One wishing to cultivate love of God should discriminate about food; for, as the Upanishads say, when the food is pure the mind becomes pure. The gross part of food helps to build up the body, and the subtle force lodged in it manufactures thought. The influence of food on thought is easily observed: a heavy meal induces mental indolence, and after drinking a large quantity of liquor one finds it difficult to control the mind. Certain kinds of food excite the mind and the senses, and other kinds dull them; a vegetarian diet is helpful. Dirt and dust must be removed from food, which should also be free from any contact with the saliva of another person. Lastly, food cooked or served by an impure person adversely affects the devotee's mind. Therefore a lover of God who develops a sensitive mind should be careful about food. (Sankaracharya gives a wider meaning to food: it means not only what goes into the mouth, but also what is taken by the other sense-organs besides the tongue. The objects of the senses should be conducive to the cultivation of the spiritual life; therefore discrimination should be applied to what we see, touch, hear, smell, and eat.)

Second, the devotee should control extreme desires for material objects. Objects are helpful only in so far as they further the spiritual life. They are means to an end, and not an end in themselves. The desire to possess them should be suppressed if they lead to entanglement in the world.

Third, the devotee of God should practise devotion unflaggingly. As progress is never made at a constant level, he should remain undisturbed by the ebb and flow of his spiritual life. During a period of ebb, he must hold to the progress he has already made, and during the flow he should move forward swiftly. What a person does or thinks now is the result of his past practices, and thus he can build for the future through his present practices. By practice the mind can be made to flow uninterruptedly toward God, as oil flows uninterruptedly when it is poured from one jar to another. Love for the ideal makes practice easy and pleasant. If the devotee feels dryness of heart, he can remove it with the help of devotional music.

Fourth, one should learn unselfishness by doing good to others. The selfish man can never cultivate divine love. The Hindu scriptures speak of five unselfish actions, called the "fivefold sacrifice," to be performed by a pious householder. These have already been described.[1]

Fifth, one should always practise purity, which comprises truthfulness, straightforwardness, compassion, non-injury, and charity. God is truth and reveals Himself to the truthful; it is said that if one never deviates from the truth for twelve years, one's words become infallible. Straightforwardness means the simplicity and the guilelessness of the innocent child, who is specially favoured of God. By means of compassion, a man controls his greed and selfishness. A devotee abstains from injuring others by thought, word, or deed. There is no virtue higher than charity; he who goes to the extent of hurting himself while helping others receives divine grace.

Sixth, one should avoid despondency. Religion is not gloominess; one does not find a melancholy saint. The cheerfulness of a devotee comes from his faith in God.

Seventh, a devotee should avoid excessive merriment, which makes the mind fickle and is always followed by sorrow. Laughter and tears are inseparable companions.

The devotee who practises these seven disciplines acquires genuine love of God.

There are two forms of divine love: preparatory and supreme. During the preparatory stage certain forms of external help are necessary. Needless to say, the aspirant must be ready for the spiritual life; he must feel a true yearning for God. Sometimes momentary impulses are mistaken for such yearn-

---

[1] See p. 69.

ing. One may feel a desire for the spiritual life when struck by a blow from the world, in the shape of the death of a near and dear one, or loss of money. But one generally recovers from such a shock. He is a true devotee of God who, though he may possess all kinds of material goods, is not interested in them because he is aware of their impermanent and unsubstantial nature. Such an aspirant, pure in thought, word, and deed, seeks the help of a spiritual teacher. God no doubt dwells in all men and is their inner guide. But since at the outset a man's impure thoughts usually distort the divine voice, he needs a guide to show him the right path. The teacher quickens the spiritual awakening; a candle is lighted from another lighted candle. Religious history shows that even the greatest saints and mystics have taken help from a qualified teacher; the mere study of books is not enough.

A teacher must be properly qualified and should possess knowledge of the scriptures in order to dispel students' doubts. He must have direct experience of God, the most important qualification. Free from sinfulness and selfish motives, he must be "like an ocean of mercy which knows no reason." With infinite patience and infinite love he unfolds the disciple's heart, as the breeze opens the buds at the advent of spring. The father provides one with the physical birth, but the teacher with the spiritual birth. The student should approach the teacher with respect, in a spirit of service, and ask him intelligent questions. The meeting of a qualified student with a God-like teacher—as when Peter met with Christ, or Vivekananda with Ramakrishna—is a wonderful event in the spiritual world. The ideal teacher here described is indeed rare. But one may also derive benefit from a less perfect guide. As the mind of the pupil becomes purer, he finds that God—who dwells in everyone's heart—is guiding him on his spiritual path.

Bhakti-yoga accepts the doctrine of God's incarnation.[2] Our human constitution and nature make us seek God in a man. However we may try to think of Him as omnipotent, omniscient, eternal, and infinite, we do not succeed, with our limited minds, in forming an adequate picture of Him. Through practice of spiritual disciplines we gradually transcend our human nature, and God as spirit becomes evident to us; but in the meantime we need to think of God through a human symbol. According to Hindu mythology, when the earth was covered with water and peopled with sea-creatures, God became incarnated as a fish for the benefit of the fish-world. Then as other forms of life evolved God became incarnated as a turtle, as a boar, as a creature half lion and half man, as a hunter, as an ethical man, and so on. The Bhagavad Gita says that whenever virtue subsides and wickedness prevails, God manifests Himself as a God-man. He is born from time to time to establish virtue and destroy evil. Ramakrishna said: "When a huge tidal-wave comes, all the little brooks and ponds become full to the brim without much effort; so when a God-man is born, a tidal-wave of spirituality breaks upon the world and the very air becomes filled with spiritual fervour." A divine incarnation has always received the homage of humanity; that man alone who has transcended the limitations of his human nature does not need to worship an incarnation.

A God-man can transmit spirituality to a seeker by a touch or a look or a mere wish. But a less perfect teacher employs more tangible methods. He often uses a sacred word called mantra, charged with spiritual power; by repeating such a word and contemplating its meaning, the aspirant gradually attains to perfection. As the great oak lies hidden in a small acorn, so also is God with His endless attributes hidden in His

[2] See also pp. 30–31.

name; God and His name are inseparable. The power of God's name has been recognized by all the great faiths of the world.

Bhakti-yoga speaks of worshipping substitutes of God. A devotee "joins his mind with devotion" to a symbol which is not God, taking it to be God. The Vedas speak of the mind, the sun, and other substitutes; the worship of these is a form of ritual and produces appropriate results. Then there is worship of holy images in which there is a special manifestation of God. Images are accepted by Hinduism, Mahayana Buddhism, and Roman Catholicism. Moslems visit the graves of the saints and martyrs in order to awaken God-consciousness. There are two ways in which images and substitutes can be used for worship. If the devotee worships them as God, for a selfish purpose, then he may be called an idolater; he obtains a limited result. But if he worships God through them, he develops love of God and ultimately attains liberation. To worship the image as God is to bring down God to the level of a physical object; but such worship is neither wicked nor sinful. To worship, on the other hand, God through the help of an image is to spiritualize the image itself. Some of the world's greatest saints have worshipped God through images.

A very important factor in the path of devotion is the doctrine of the Ishta, or Chosen Ideal, especially developed by Hinduism. The Lord is one, but infinite are His manifestations. Different religious sects worship different manifestations, suited to their needs and temperaments. One important discipline of bhakti-yoga is that a devotee of God must not hate or criticize the objects of worship of other sects; he must not even hear criticism of them. The ideal devotee is he who possesses an extensive sympathy and power of appreciation and at the same time intense love. But such a soul is rare. The liberal and tolerant person is generally devoid of intensity of religious feeling, and the so-called intense lover of God is often

found to acquire every particle of his love by hating the ideals
of others who differ from him in their religious outlook. The
goal of bhakti-yoga is to blend both breadth and intensity of
love, and Hinduism lays down the doctrine of the Chosen
Ideal to accomplish this purpose. While each religious sect
presents only one ideal of its own, Vedanta opens to mankind
an infinite number of doors to enter into the inner shrine of
the Lord and places before the world an almost inexhaustible
array of ideals, each of them a manifestation of the Eternal
Lord. Though a devotee must respect all of these ideals, he
remains completely loyal to his own. The young sapling must
be protected by hedges until it grows into a tree; the tender
plant of spirituality must not be exposed to a constant change
of ideas and ideals, or it will wither away. Many pseudo-lib-
erals are seen to feed their idle curiosity with a continuous
succession of different ideals; but a true devotee is like the
pearl-oyster of the Hindu fable, which comes to the surface to
catch a raindrop, and then dives deep to the sea-bed to lie
there until it has succeeded in fashioning out of it a beautiful
pearl. Devotion to one ideal is absolutely necessary for the
beginner in the practice of divine love. A Hindu mystic said:
"Enjoy the sweetness of all, keep company with all, respect all
names, say yea, yea to all, but never budge an inch from your
own seat." Then if the devotee is sincere and patient, out of
the little seed of devotion will come a gigantic tree, like the
Indian banyan, sending out branch after branch and root after
root to all sides, till it covers the entire field of religion. At the
end, the genuine devotee realizes that He who is his own
Chosen Ideal is also worshipped as the Chosen Ideal by all
other sects, under different names and forms; He is the all-
pervading Brahman, too, contemplated by non-dualists.

A few words may be said regarding the practice of concentration by a lover of God. The object of his concentration is

naturally his Chosen Ideal, either an incarnation or any form
of the Personal God. The Bhagavad Gita says that a devotee
should practise concentration in solitude, and in a clean spot
fix his seat—a firm seat, neither too high nor too low. He
should not eat too much or too little, and should follow the
middle path about rest, work, and sleep. Intense austerity dries
up the heart and prevents the growth of love. As the devotee
meditates on his ideal, he first visualizes indistinctly only parts
of His body; the outside world is still very real to him. As the
meditation deepens, the figure of the ideal becomes more real,
and the physical world dreamlike. At last the physical world
completely disappears and the Chosen Ideal appears as a living person, speaking and giving guidance to the devotee. Even
when the devotee comes back to consciousness of the phenomenal world, it is not the same world to him as is seen by
others. Henceforth, in whatever manner he lives and works, his
mind is always inclined to God, as the needle of a compass always points to the north.

After practising the disciplines of the preparatory stage, the
devotee begins to feel supreme love for God. This supreme
love is based upon renunciation. There is no real yoga without
renunciation. Karma-yoga asks the aspirant to renounce the

fruit of his action; raja-yoga, his attachment to nature; and
jnana-yoga, the entire physical universe. But the renunciation
practised by a lover of God, as stated before, is easy, natural,
and smooth. As he tastes the bliss of God his attachment to
lower pleasures drops away without much effort. Gradually
he loses all interest in forms, rituals, the scriptures, images,
temples, and churches. He directs all his impulses to God and
makes them more intense. Bhakti-yoga does not say, "Give
up"; it only says, "Love; love the highest," and anything that
is lower will naturally drop away. To a devotee, God is the
only object of love; all other objects reflect God's beauty. "He

shining, everything shines; by His light all are lighted." Thus
supreme love for God loosens attachment to worldly objects.
The blessed soul who has attained this ecstatic love is not interested in name and form. He sees no distinction between one
man and another, but beholds God in all; through every face
shines his Beloved. He alone knows the meaning of the brotherhood of men.

Supreme love manifests itself in various ways through the
feelings, thoughts, conduct, and actions of the devotee. Out of
this love comes reverence, which enables the devotee to rise
above friction and to respect all life. He experiences an intense
pleasure in all things associated with the Lord, and when God
is not perceived his suffering knows no bounds; he is greatly
disturbed in the company of the worldly-minded. Not a sour-
tempered ascetic, he regards life as beautiful and worth living
on account of this divine love. Gradually his whole nature
changes and he feels as if he were losing his identity in his
beloved God. Many lovers of God, however, preserve their
individuality for the sake of worshipping Him and serving His
creatures; they are free, nevertheless, from attachment to the
world, for they realize that all things belong to the Lord. They
love the universe because it is all His.

Swami Vivekananda likened supreme love of God to a triangle. The first angle of love is that it knows no bargaining.
Love does not seek anything in return, not even salvation; it is
love for love's sake. The devotee loves God because He is
lovable; he cannot help loving God any more than one can
help loving a beautiful sunset. In neither case is there any
question of seeking something in return. The very thought of
love makes the lover happy. The second angle is that supreme
love knows no fear. A devotee does not love God for fear of
punishment. As long as there is any fear in the heart there is
no real love, for love conquers fear; they cannot coexist. And

3 the third angle is that love knows no rival; in it the lover beholds the embodiment of his highest ideal. He finds in his beloved God the culmination of beauty, sublimity, and power.
The devotee who has attained such a lofty state of love does
not seek any proof of God's existence. God, as love, is self-evident. He is no longer sought in temples or churches, in heaven,
or in the scriptures. There is no place where He does not exist.

Love-intoxicated mystics have tried to express this transcendental love in human terms. Thus we read of the devotees'
loving God as the Master and the King, as the Friend, as the
Child, as the Bridegroom, or as the divine Sweetheart. One
test of the growth of love is the narrowing of the distance between the lover and the beloved. The love of God finds its
fulfilment when the devotee can love Him with the same passion and intensity, with the same self-surrender and careless
abandon, with which a woman loves her sweetheart. But such
love does not arise when there is the slightest desire in the
devotee's heart, not even the desire for freedom, salvation,
or Nirvana. The whole universe is full of love and love alone;
that is how it appears to the lover of God. The possessor of
such love is eternally blessed, eternally happy. It is he who can
cure the rudeness, selfishness, and cruelty of a loveless world.

The peculiar trend of Hindu speculation is toward the realization of the universal which includes all particulars. Thus
the Upanishads exhort one to realize Brahman, or the universal spirit, and know all things as its manifestations. The God
of bhakti-yoga is the one generalized abstract Person, in loving
whom one loves the whole universe and all created beings. The
visible universe is God made manifest through a multitude of
names and forms. Therefore if a man loves God, he loves the
world and offers loving service to everyone, to every life, to
every creature. Love of God is the spiritual basis of the social
service practised by dualists. To a devotee, everything is sa-

cred, because all are God's children, His body, His manifestations. The nearer one approaches God, the more one sees all
things in Him.

The culmination of this intense, all-absorbing love is perfect
self-surrender based upon the conviction that nothing happens
which is against the devotee's welfare. Thus the lover of God
welcomes misery, pain, and even the terror of death. This total
self-resignation to the will of God is indeed a worthier prize
than all the glory of heroic performances. A lover of God is
willing to sacrifice his body, if needed, in the service of any of
the Lord's creatures; Buddha is said to have offered his life
out of compassion in order to save the life of a goat. A devotee does not injure an animal, because the latter, too, is
God's creature; a Hindu mystic of modern times once welcomed a venomous snake as a messenger from his Beloved. In
this evanescent world where everything comes to an end, the
devotee of God makes the highest use of life by holding it at
the service of others. The consciousness of the body, which
generally breeds selfishness, does not offer him any obstacle;
he knows positively that his body is God's instrument and
should be used to benefit his fellow creatures. This is the true
self-surrender. "Let things come as they may," a devotee says;
"Thy will be done." Through self-surrender and love, a devotee knows the mysteries of the Lord, becomes absorbed in
Him, and thus attains immortality.

VII.

Spiritual Disciplines III (Jnana-Yoga)

Philosophical Yoga [handwritten]

JNANA-YOGA, discussed in Vedanta,[1] is the discipline of philosophical discrimination by which jnana, or the knowledge of Brahman, is attained. A Hindu philosopher once said about Vedanta: "I shall state in half a couplet what has been described in a million books: Brahman alone is real; the phenomenal universe is unreal; the living being is none other than Brahman." Jnana-yoga establishes the sole reality of Brahman.

The ultimate oneness of the Godhead, living beings, and the universe is emphasized by Sankaracharya as the essence and conclusion of Vedanta as expounded in the Upanishads, the Bhagavad Gita, and the *Brahma-Sutras.* Sankaracharya, popularly called Sankara, was born, according to modern scholars, during the eighth century after Christ. The year of his birth is given as A.D. 788 and that of his death as 820. He belonged to a sect of austere, scholarly, and industrious brahmins of Malabar in South India. After completing the study of the Vedas, he embraced the monastic life at an early age, devoted himself to the practice of spiritual disciplines, and was soon recognized as the leading philosopher and mystic of India, and a reformer of Hinduism. Before his death at Kedarnath in the Himalayas,

[1] In this chapter, the use of the word *Vedanta* is limited to apply to the philosophy of non-dualism. There are two other interpretations of Vedanta, namely, qualified non-dualism and dualism, whose chief exponents are respectively Ramanuja and Madhva.

at the age of thirty-two, he had travelled the length and breadth of India and established monasteries at the four corners of the country. Sankara lived during the decadent period of Buddhism when India was torn with sectarianism and religious conflict, causing bewilderment to earnest seekers of truth. In open debate and through his now well-known commentaries on the scriptures he refuted the views of his opponents and established non-dualism as the ultimate teaching of the Vedas. It is refreshing to contemplate the serenity and unshakable assurance of Sankara's philosophy amidst the polemics of his time. It may be safely stated that Sankara's interpretation of Hinduism is, even today, India's original and unsurpassed contribution to the philosophical thought of the world. He established the fact that ultimate reality, though supramental, need not remain a dogma of religion or the private vision of mysticism, but that it is a philosophical truth which may be demonstrated by reason and which is supported by universal experience. Despite ceaseless activity, he found time to write, in addition to his more famous works, several small philosophical treatises and to compose hymns in praise of the Hindu deities. In Sankara one finds the unusual combination of a philosopher and a poet, an astute thinker and a clear writer, a savant and a saint, a mystic and a religious reformer, a debater of rare forensic power and a passionate lover of God. He is one of the brightest stars in the philosophical and religious firmament of India.

The knowledge of Vedanta, like all other forms of genuine spiritual knowledge, has been transmitted through a succession of teachers. Books may give information or even mental stimulation, but the guru, or teacher, helps to awaken spiritual consciousness. Naturally, a high degree of perfection is expected of the teacher, whose qualifications have already been mentioned.[2] The disciple approaches the benign guru and says to him, in the words of Sankara: "Save me from death, afflicted as I am by the unquenchable fire of the forest of the world, a fire which blazes violently on account of the wind of the wicked deeds performed by me in my previous lives. Save me, who am terrified and so seek refuge in thee; for I know of no other with whom to take shelter. How I shall cross the ocean of phenomenal existence, what is to be my fate, and what means I should adopt—as to these I know nothing. Condescend to save me, and describe at length how to put an end to repeated births and deaths, fraught with suffering and frustration." "Fear not, O blessed one," the distressed disciple is reassured by the guru. "There is no death for you. There is a means of crossing the ocean of apparently interminable births and deaths in this transitory world. The very way the sages have trod heretofore, I shall point out to you. It is through the touch of ignorance that you, who are the supreme self, find yourself under the bondage of the non-self, whence alone proceeds the round of births and deaths. The fire of knowledge, kindled by discrimination between the self and non-self, consumes ignorance with its effects."

The successful study of Vedanta presupposes a sort of intuitive knowledge of the limitations and misery inevitable in the life of the embodied soul: there is suffering in birth, disease, old age, and in death. One believing in progress and ultimate perfection in the phenomenal world will not be able to grasp the essence of non-dualistic Vedanta. Furthermore, the student of non-dualism must be equipped with proper qualifications. True knowledge does not consist of mere information; it must transform a man's character and inspire the activities of his daily life. An objective attitude, faithful adherence to facts, and intellectual honesty may be adequate for scientific knowl-

[2] See p. 108.

edge, but Vedanta requires much more. The four cardinal disciplines of Vedanta are as follows:

(1) Discrimination between the real and the unreal. This discrimination springs from the intuitive conviction that the eternal and unchanging Brahman alone is real, and all other objects are transitory and unreal. The student is born, as it were, with this conviction on account of his having been previously disillusioned, by experiences in previous lives, about the reality of the happiness one may expect on earth and in the heavenly worlds. Discrimination is the first and foremost discipline; without it the next discipline cannot be practised.

(2) Renunciation. This means non-attachment to all pleasures, ranging from the enjoyment of the tangible objects found on earth to that of the happiness a virtuous soul experiences in heaven. All actions are by nature finite; therefore their results, too, are finite. Such impermanent factors of an action as the doer, his body and sense-organs, and the physical accessories he employs, cannot produce a permanent result. A student of Vedanta must be endowed not only with a keen power of intellect in order to discriminate between the real and the unreal, but also with a stern power of will to give up the unreal. Too often the unreal appears to us in the guise of the real, and too often we lack the power to renounce even what we know to be unreal.

(3) Next comes a group of six virtues, namely, control of the body and the senses; control of the mind; prevention of the sense-organs, once they are controlled, from drifting back to their respective objects; forbearance; complete concentration; and faith. Self-control, as already stated, must not be confused with torture or mortification of the body.[3] Through the practice of forbearance, the student remains unruffled by heat and cold, pleasure and pain, and the other pairs of opposites. By

[3] See pp. 76–77.

means of concentration he keeps his mind on the ideal. Faith
enables him to listen, with respect, to the instruction of the
teacher and the injunctions of the scriptures. This faith is not
mechanical belief, but an affirmative attitude of mind regarding the existence of reality, as opposed to a negative and cyn-
ical attitude. The man who always doubts comes to grief.

(4) Longing for freedom. A serious student of Vedanta
realizes through rational investigation and actual experience
that a man attached to the world is a bound creature and
never really happy. Thus a genuine aspirant longs for freedom;
but this longing must not be confused with the momentary
yearning created by frustration or worldly loss. True renunciation and longing for freedom are the two vital disciplines
through which the other disciplines bear fruit. Without these,
even ethical virtues create only a mirage of spirituality. The
Upanishads state that the knowledge of the self reveals itself
only to one who longs for it intensely.

Sankaracharya lays emphasis on bhakti as a means to the
realization of freedom, and defines it as a single-minded longing for truth. Without this emotional urge the aspirant often
becomes lost in the wilderness of philosophical speculation or
seeks satisfaction in intellectual gymnastics.

The path of knowledge is steep and austere, and the search
for impersonal reality is extremely difficult for those who are
constantly aware of their duties to the world. This path, therefore, is usually pursued by monks, who have renounced the
world. The monastic ideal of India is as ancient as the Hindu
spiritual culture itself, though it received added impetus at the
time of Buddha. Sankaracharya, in his commentaries on the
Upanishads, the Bhagavad Gita, and the *Brahma-Sutras*, emphatically asserts the incompatibility of the unitive knowledge
of Brahman with any kind of activity, ritualistic or philanthropic, because the latter cannot be dissociated from the triple

factors of the doer, the instrument of action, and the result of action. Thus he is convinced that the non-dual Brahman can be realized only by all-renouncing sannyasins, and not by householders, if the latter are true to their dharma.

To the qualified pupil who has properly approached the preceptor, the latter gives instruction so that he may overcome ignorance and realize the oneness of existence. It is explained to the pupil that on account of maya, or nescience, Brahman, that is to say, pure consciousness, appears as the conditioned Brahman or the omnipotent, omniscient, and omnipresent Creator, Preserver, and Destroyer of the universe. From the conditioned Brahman evolve the five subtle elements of akasa, air, fire, water, and earth, which, becoming gross, produce the universe and all the physical objects contained in it. Under the influence of the same nescience, Brahman appears as the individual soul, who is endowed with a mind, a body, sense-organs, vital breaths, and is a victim of birth and death. All this, as explained before, is called in Vedanta the illusory superimposition of the unreal upon the real. This superimposition does not change in the least the nature of pure consciousness, just as the illusory water of the mirage does not affect the desert. From the relative standpoint, however, the conditioned Brahman is the cause of the universe: maya is the material cause, and pure intelligence the efficient cause.

Next, the teacher explains the refutation or negation of this illusory superimposition. As a snake perceived in a rope is found, after proper investigation, to be nothing but the rope, he says, so also the world of unreal entities beginning with ignorance and ending in the material universe and physical bodies and the conditioned Brahman—all superimposed upon Reality through ignorance—is finally realized to be nothing but pure Brahman. Causality itself, as also time and space, belongs to the realm of phenomena and cannot affect Brah-

man. Brahman alone exists; the universe apart from Brahman
is non-existent. Vedanta is neither pantheism, which would
tacitly admit of Brahman's *becoming* the universe, nor is it il-
lusionism, which would accept the reality of a maya under
whose influence Brahman projects the universe. From the ultimate standpoint there is neither projection nor becoming. Pure
consciousness is immutable.

According to non-dualists, the true nature of Brahman is
realized through the method of negation. Every act of negation
leaves behind a positive residuum. Thus, when the snake is
negated, there remains the rope, and when the rope is negated
something else remains. After all the changing superimpositions
have been negated, there remains being, or sat, which is pure
consciousness. It may be contended, as certain of the Buddhist
philosophers have argued, that when the process of negation
is carried to its logical conclusion, what remains is a void; thus
ultimate reality is a void, or non-existence. In reply it is said
that there must be a perceiving consciousness which is aware
of the void. And this consciousness is Brahman. He who doubts
or denies this fact is himself Brahman.

What is the process by which a student realizes his oneness
with Brahman? The teacher instructs him about the four great
Vedic statements asserting this unity directly experienced by
the Vedic seers and subsequently explained by philosophers:
"That thou art," "I am Brahman," "This self is Brahman,"
and "Brahman is consciousness." Let us try to understand the
meaning of the first statement, "That thou art" (*tattvamasi*),
with which many people in the West have now become fa-
miliar. The direct meaning of the word *That* comprises the
conditioned Brahman (associated with the upadhis, or limiting adjuncts of creation, preservation, and destruction, and
endowed with omniscience, lordship, omnipotence, and similar
attributes) and pure consciousness, which is its unrelated sub-

stratum. Likewise the direct meaning of the word *thou* comprises the jiva or individualized soul (associated with the limiting adjuncts of the body, mind, and the sense-organs and endowed with such traits as little knowledge, little power, and dependence) and pure consciousness, which is its unrelated substratum. But there is also an implied meaning of the words *That* and *thou,* namely, pure consciousness itself, unassociated with any limiting adjuncts. It is common practice to explain a statement through its implied meaning when the direct meaning contradicts actual experience: when we see that a red-hot iron ball burns something, we say that the direct agent of burning is the iron; but the implied, though real, agent is fire, unassociated with the iron; again, in the statement "He spent the night on a sleepless pillow," the word *sleepless* does not refer to the pillow but to the person who used the pillow. Similarly, in the Vedic statement "That thou art," the word *art* denotes the identity of *That* and *thou,* which directly refer to the conditioned Brahman and the embodied soul respectively. But this identity is obviously absurd, since they are poles asunder.[4] Therefore we must explain the statement by its implied meaning. The identity is really based upon the pure consciousness which is the unrelated substratum of both. The limiting adjuncts in both cases are the creation of ignorance and therefore unreal; so these must be discarded. Therefore the statement "That thou art" really conveys a transcendental experience of oneness which is beyond the body, mind, senses, and ego and the sensations associated with them. When a person realizes his oneness with Brahman, he is oblivious of the idea that he is an embodied being.

Next, the teacher exhorts the disciple to meditate on his real nature:

4 See p. 36.

"That which is beyond caste and creed, family and lineage, which is devoid of name and form, merit and demerit, that which transcends space, time, and sense-objects—that Brahman art thou. Meditate on this in thy mind.

"That which is free from birth, growth, maturity, decline, infirmity, and death; that which is indestructible; that which is the cause of the projection, maintenance, and dissolution of the universe—that Brahman art thou. Meditate on this in thy mind.

"That which is free from duality; that which is infinite and indestructible; that which is supreme, eternal, and undying; that which is taintless—that Brahman art thou. Meditate on this in thy mind.

"That beyond which there is nothing; which shines above maya and is infinitely greater than the universe; the innermost self of all; the One without a second; existence-knowledge-bliss absolute; infinite and immutable—that Brahman art thou. Meditate on this in thy mind."

As the disciple reflects deeply on the teacher's instruction, he gradually frees himself from the superimpositions which, like chains, bind one to the world. Vedanta speaks of three strong chains, namely, the observance of social formalities, over-engrossment in the scriptures, and undue attention to the physical body. The more the mind is established in Brahman, the less it feels attached to the physical world. The discipline must be practised, without interruption, as long as even a dream-like perception of the phenomenal universe and the physical body remains. Even after the truth has been known, there often lingers the strong, primordial, and stubborn notion of ego, which can be destroyed only by living for some time in a state of constant communion with Brahman. Sloth and inadvertence are great enemies of the spiritual life, more harmful than many notorious sins. Inadvertence, delusion, egotism, bondage, and suffering are the successive links in the chain of the worldly life.

Having reflected, by means of suitable reasoning, on the instruction of the teacher, the student next devotes himself to meditation on Brahman, which means that his mind constantly dwells on a stream of ideas identical with the conception of the non-dual Brahman, to the exclusion of such foreign ideas as body, senses, mind, and ego. As he meditates on his oneness with Brahman, there arises within him a mental state which makes him feel that he is Brahman—ever free, ever blissful, and ever illumined. This mental state gradually destroys his ignorance and doubts about Brahman. Yet even now for him Brahman is only a mental state or wave in the mind. With the deepening of meditation, the mind, which is a manifestation of ignorance and a form of matter, is destroyed, and in the absence of the reflecting medium, the Brahman reflected in the mind is absorbed in the supreme Brahman, which shines alone; it is like the reverting to the sun of its reflection in a dish of water when the dish is destroyed. Thus the subject and the object, pure consciousness and the individualized consciousness, become one. This unity, indescribable in words, is known only to him who has experienced it.

Later Vedantists have recommended the practice of the disciplines prescribed by Patanjali in the *Yoga-sutras* for the attainment of the knowledge of Brahman through samadhi, or total absorption. These disciplines will be discussed in the next section. There are two kinds of samadhi. The experience of the one, in which the aspirant retains the distinction of the knower, knowledge, and the object of knowledge, may be likened to looking at a clay elephant and remaining conscious of the clay that permeates the figure. In this samadhi one retains consciousness of the individual soul, the body, and the world, and at the same time sees them all as permeated by

Brahman, or pure consciousness. In the other samadhi, the I-consciousness is totally obliterated, and there no longer remains any distinction between knower, knowledge, and the object of knowledge. This experience may be likened to the dissolving of a lump of salt in the water of the ocean, from which it was originally extracted; the salt cannot be separated any more from the water.

The need of vigilance is imperative at every step of the spiritual life. The obstacles which beset the path until the goal is reached are generally created by the mind's inability to rest in Brahman, though it has become somewhat detached from the world. The four main obstacles are torpidity, distraction, attachment, and enjoyment of bliss. Often the student, while practising meditation, falls into a state of sleep because his mind is without a support either in Brahman or in the world. The remedy for this is devotional music, study of the scriptures, a visit to holy places, or some such stimulating spiritual exercise. Second, the mind, while practising meditation, feels distracted by ideas, for the most part petty and inconsequential, which flit through the mind like the dust particles dancing in a sunbeam coming through a chink in the door or the wall into a dark room. They are often the result of the aspirant's futile talk and physical movements when not engaged in meditation. The remedy is in the pacification of the mind through patience and perseverance. Third, the mind may suddenly be seized by a violent attachment to a long-forgotten experience lying nestled in the subconscious mind; this can be overcome by means of stern discrimination and will-power. And last, one may feel quite satisfied with the enjoyment of an inferior bliss or a foretaste of the joy of Brahman, and be unwilling to make any further effort to reach the ultimate goal. This is explained by the illustration of a man who has heard of a treasure box hidden under a stone. As he approaches the place, he is challenged by a powerful dragon. A life-and-death struggle follows and at last the dragon is killed. But the man feels so exhilarated by the destruction of his enemy that he dances about in joy, forgetting all about the treasure. A spiritual seeker, too, becomes extremely delighted when, after a stubborn fight, he suppresses certain passions and attachments, and forgets to go further in order to realize his freedom. Sometimes the enjoyment of the delight arising from supraphysical experiences makes the aspirant forget his goal. The remedy for this obstacle is that the aspirant should not permit his mind to dwell long on any transient experience. He must detach himself from all forms of reflected bliss, however alluring they may appear, and not stop till the goal is reached. With sincerity and zeal, earnestness and perseverance, patience and love for the ideal, the devotee finally overcomes all obstacles, great and small, through the blessings of his teacher and the grace of God: he realizes his oneness with Brahman.

Now the imprisoned lion is freed from its cage and can roam again in the forest, its natural habitat; the bound soul has attained freedom while dwelling in the body. The characteristics of a free soul have already been described.[5] Himself released from fear, he gives the assurance of fearlessness to all. Himself free from worry, he does not cause worry to anyone. He lives, works, and dies under the spell of the soul's immortality, nonduality, and divinity. But whether endowed with a physical body or not, he has entered into a realm of new consciousness, from which he directs his activities for the welfare of all. By the birth of such a person, as a Hindu poet has said, his family becomes purified, his mother blessed among women, and the earth sanctified for having nourished a worthy soul.

[5] See pp. 53–56.

VIII.

Spiritual Disciplines IV (Raja-Yoga)

study and control of mind

LET US now consider the spiritual discipline prescribed in raja-yoga, which devotes itself to the study of the mind and its control. In the *Yoga-sutras,* these disciplines have been systematized by the ancient Hindu philosopher and seer Patanjali. The method of raja-yoga, practical and rational, has been tested again and again by Indian yogis. Its technique can be followed in varying degrees by all, irrespective of their religion, in their practice of meditation and concentration.

The study of the mind is more difficult than the study of the external world, because the states of the mind constantly change. Furthermore, in this yoga the observer, the object, and the instrument of observation are all different states of the mind. Still another difficulty arises from the fact that most of us have been trained from childhood to observe and analyse only the outer world of nature and not the inner world of the mind. In the West the systematic study of physics and astronomy began much earlier than that of psychology. What we are now to deal with is the phenomenon of the mind studying itself through the mind. The powers of the mind are generally scattered; but they can be concentrated and thus be made to become a powerful searchlight to illumine the whole of a man's inner self.

All great achievements of human civilization, for instance,

the cathedral of Chartres, the Taj Mahal, the caves of Ajanta, Michelangelo's statue of Moses, the dome of Saint Peter's, the *Republic* of Plato, or Einstein's theory of relativity, were first conceived in the mind and then tangibly expressed in the outer world. Before being relegated to oblivion by the processes of nature, they also will have been discarded by the mind. Concentration is the sole method by which one can develop the innate power of the mind and learn the secrets not only of the outer but also of the inner world. Scientists observe facts to arrive at reality; but mere observation does not constitute the scientific method; the facts must be properly studied. Men had seen apples falling for untold ages, but Sir Isaac Newton's reflection on this fact resulted in the formulation of the law of gravitation. Concentration of the mind should be practised by all creative people who wish to succeed in their work. In the realm of religious experience its value is immeasurable.

Patanjali has defined yoga as the restraining of the mind from taking various forms (vrittis). Let us try to form a general idea of the mind according to Hindu philosophers and psychologists. Consisting of subtle material elements, the mind is the inner organ of apperception, as opposed to the outer organs by which the objects of the external world are perceived. It functions in four different ways and is given names appropriate to its functions, such as manas (mind), buddhi (intellect), chitta (mind-stuff), and aham (ego).[1] The Upanishads give the following functions of the inner organ: desire, determination, doubt, faith, lack of faith, steadfastness, lack of steadfastness, shame, intelligence, and fear. According to Hindu psychologists, the inner and outer organs, as also physical objects, are not essentially different from one another, because they all consist of gross or subtle matter. The insentient sense-organs and mind derive the power of illumining objects

[1] See pp. 37–38.

from atman, or the inner spirit, which is the source of all light.

How does a perception arise? The sense-organs, through the nerves, carry the sensations of external objects to the brain centres, where they are presented to the inner organ. One aspect of the inner organ, the manas, or mind, creates doubt regarding the nature of these sensations; the buddhi, or intellect, comes to a decision by comparing them with the sensations stored up in the chitta, or mind-stuff; then the aham, or ego, plays its part. Thus it is that one says: "I see a cow," or "I hear a bus." But, as already stated, the inner organ, which by nature is material and non-intelligent, cannot function unless activated by the light of atman.

The nature of mental states is influenced by the three gunas —sattva, rajas, and tamas—which constitute the mind as well as all material objects, gross or subtle. That is why the same object can create different feelings in different minds. A beautiful woman, for instance, may be regarded either with pain or with joy by the disappointed or successful suitor in whom rajas prevails, and with calmness by a saint whose mind has a preponderance of sattva; she hardly evokes any sentiment in a mind full of tamas.

One does not generally see what lies deep in the mind, because its surface is constantly agitated by impressions from the outside world. If the water of a lake is muddy or disturbed, one does not see the bottom. But when the mud settles and the ripples subside, an object lying in the depths is plainly visible. As the water is clear by nature, mud being extraneous to it, so the mind is by nature translucent and capable of revealing the true nature of atman. But it appears to have lost its clarity on account of an excess of rajas and tamas, which may be controlled through proper spiritual disciplines. The uncontrolled sense-organs, coming in contact with physical objects, constantly draw the mind outward and create waves. It is the aim of yoga to detach the mind from the sense-organs and check its outward tendencies. Only then can it reflect the true nature of atman.

The ordinary states of the mind are "darkened" or "scattered." The darkened mind, filled with tamas, is dull and passive. The scattered mind, with an excess of rajas, is restless. No higher perceptions are possible through either of these states. By the disciplines of yoga the darkened mind and the scattered mind can be "gathered" and made "one-pointed." Then alone does the yogi attain total absorption, or samadhi, and realize the true nature of his self, as when the waves subside, one sees the bottom of the lake. But an ordinary man identifies himself with one or another state of the mind and experiences grief, fear, or happiness.

According to raja-yoga, the waves of the mind can be controlled by practice and non-attachment. The unceasing struggle to keep the mind perfectly restrained is called practice. Though at first difficult, it becomes easy through protracted effort accompanied by intense love for the goal. Non-attachment means the control of yearning for any object unrelated to the goal the yogi has set out to realize. This goal is the freedom of the soul, and non-attachment thus means the repression of desire for all such material objects of the phenomenal universe as one experiences on earth, and also for those which are realized in the heavenly worlds, about which one reads in the scriptures. Both kinds of objects are impermanent, being subject to time, space, and the law of causation.

Various disciplines are prescribed by Patanjali to quiet the mind. Here is one: A student of yoga should cultivate an attitude of friendship toward those who are happy, mercy toward those who are unhappy, gladness toward the good, and indifference toward the evil. A yogi still struggling for perfection does not become a social reformer. Jesus said to a disciple:

"Follow me; and let the dead bury their dead. Come and follow me," or "For ye have the poor always with you; but me ye have not always." A yogi tries to redress evils happening before his eyes, if he sees them, but he certainly does not create new distractions by going out to seek them. He devotes himself to the spiritual welfare of others after he has attained illumination. The mind can also be quieted by regulated breathing, or through concentration on light, or on a pleasant dream or on any delectable object.

A further discipline for quieting the mind is devotion to Isvara, or God. Isvara is defined by Patanjali as "a special Person, untouched by misery, actions and their results, and desires." Omniscient and not limited by time, "He is the teacher of even the ancient teachers." The word that signifies God is Aum. By repeating it and meditating on its meaning, the aspirant develops introspection and overcomes such obstructions to the spiritual life as "disease, mental laziness, doubt, lack of enthusiasm, lethargy, clinging to sense-enjoyments, false perception, non-attaining of concentration, and falling away from concentration when attained." Since Aum has been given a prominent place in the Hindu scriptures, a brief interpretation of the word will be appropriate.

Aum, often written *Om* (to rhyme with *home*), is the most sacred word in the Gayatri mantra, which contains the essence of the Vedic philosophy. Hindus regard this word as an effective symbol of Brahman, and give the following reason.

Every thought has a counterpart in a word or sound; the word and the thought are inseparable. The external part of a thing is the word and the internal part of the same thing is what we may call the thought. The same thought may be expressed by different words or sounds. Though the sounds vary, yet the relation between the sounds and the thoughts is a natural one. This relation is effective only if there is a real connexion between the thing signified and the signifying symbol; otherwise the symbol will never be universally accepted. When that natural connexion exists, the symbol, when it is used, recalls the thing signified.

According to Patanjali, there is a unique relation between the Godhead and the word *Aum*. Though there are hundreds of words to signify the Godhead and each of them may be regarded as a symbol, Hindu philosophers regard Aum as the most generalized sound, the substratum and common ground of all sounds. The three letters *A, U,* and *M,* pronounced in combination as Aum, are the generalized symbols of all possible sounds. *A* (pronounced *aw* as in *dawn*) is the root sound, the key, pronounced without the tongue's touching any part of the palate; it is the least differentiated of all sounds. Again, all articulate sounds are produced in the space between the root of the tongue and the lips; the throat sound is *A,* and *M* is the final sound produced by the closing of the lips. *U* represents the rolling forward of the impulse that begins at the root of the tongue and ends at the lips. When properly pronounced, Aum represents the whole gamut of sound-production as no other word can. It is therefore the matrix of all sounds, and thus the fittest symbol of the Godhead; it is the Word, which, according to St. John, was in the beginning, was with God, and was God.

In Hinduism, Aum has been used to denote all the various ideas about reality, and has been retained through all the stages of India's religious growth. Dualists, qualified non-dualists, absolute non-dualists, and all other schools of Hinduism use Aum, one way or another, to denote ultimate reality. Even the Buddhists and Jainas, who repudiate the authority of the Vedas, have accepted the sanctity of Aum. This word, the material of all words, can be used as a sacred symbol for reality by non-Hindus as well. It is recognized by the Hindu scrip-

tures as the symbol of both the Personal God and Impersonal
Reality, or pure consciousness. The Personal God has been defined as the Creator, Preserver, and Destroyer of the universe.
The three aspects of creation, preservation, and destruction
are expressed by the three letters of Aum. *A* signifies the creative aspect of the Deity because *A* is the beginning of all
sounds. *U* signifies the preservative aspect because the sound
that is produced in the throat is preserved, as it were, by *U,*
while rolling through the mouth. Finally, *M* is the symbol of
the destructive aspect of the Deity because all sounds come to
an end when the lips are closed. There is also an undifferentiated sound which comes at the end of the utterance of Aum
and which is the symbol of pure consciousness, or the attributeless Brahman. Both the symbol and the entity signified by it are
without parts or relationships. The undifferentiated sound
finally merges in silence, which also is the final experience of
the mystics.

The Upanishads describe Aum as the symbol of the atman,
or individual soul, in its various aspects. Thus *A* is the symbol
of the atman experiencing the gross world in the waking state
through the gross body; *U* of the atman experiencing the subtle or mental world in the dream state through the subtle or
dream body; and *M* of the atman experiencing the causal
world in deep sleep through the causal body when the physical
body, the senses, and the mind are at rest. Thus Aum represents the totality of the atman's experiences in the relative
world. The undifferentiated sound that follows the particular
sounds *A, U,* and *M,* signifies the atman free from the experiences of the relative world, which is known as turiya, or pure
consciousness.

The word *Aum* was not invented by any man. It is the
primordial and uncreated sound which is heard by mystics
absorbed in contemplation, when their minds and senses are

withdrawn from the world. Through this word is revealed to them the eternal process of creation, preservation, and destruction. Ramakrishna, describing Aum both in its relative and in its transcendental aspect, said: "I give the illustration of the sound of a gong: 'tom,' t-o-m. It is the merging of the relative in the Absolute: the gross, the subtle, and the causal; waking, dream, and deep sleep, merge in turiya, or pure consciousness. The striking of the gong is like the falling of a heavy weight into a big ocean. Waves begin to rise: the relative rises from the Absolute; the causal, subtle, and gross bodies rise out of the Great Cause; from turiya emerge the states of deep sleep, dream, and waking. These waves arising from the Great Ocean merge again in the Great Ocean—from the Absolute to the relative, and from the relative to the Absolute. Therefore I give the illustration of the gong, 't-o-m.' I have clearly seen all these things. It has been revealed to me that there exists an ocean of consciousness without limit. From it are projected all things of the relative plane and in it they merge again. Millions of universes rise in the pure consciousness within the heart of man and merge in it. All this has been revealed to me; I don't know much about what your books say."

Patanjali states that there are different kinds of concentration. One can concentrate on the external, gross elements and thus learn their true nature. By means of such concentration a yogi obtains knowledge of the subtle properties of material objects, and through this knowledge he acquires what are generally known as supernatural powers, which if abused are not only lost but also bring about suffering. The concentration practised by scientists may be said to belong to this category. Through deep concentration they have discovered the inner nature of the atom and released the energy locked in it. According to Patanjali, the power acquired through such concentration enables one to obtain mastery over physical objects and enjoy material happiness. The powers released from matter may be used for both constructive and destructive purposes, depending upon the characters of the persons handling them. When used by people emotionally on the level of children and intellectually on the level of primitives, powers acquired from matter can spell disaster for humanity and bring about the downfall of physical science. Other forms of concentration, directed toward different material objects, produce corresponding results. Every yogi is required to eradicate his selfish tendencies by the practice of ethical disciplines. A genuine yogi is not interested in the enjoyment of powers, which are obstacles to the attainment of self-knowledge.

By means of concentration, the mind of a yogi acquires such unique powers that it can contemplate all objects, whether minute as an atom or huge as the solar system. Thus it can function either like a heavy scales in a warehouse or like a delicate balance in a chemical laboratory. Through the power of concentration, the yogi can withdraw his mind from all extraneous objects and identify himself solely with one object of thought. His mind becomes like a crystal, which, when placed near an object, such as a flower, identifies itself with it. The mind has now acquired one-pointedness and can penetrate deeply into the nature of the self. Thus it obtains knowledge which is far more profound than that acquired through the senses, inference, or the testimony of others. This is what is meant by direct and immediate experience, or knowledge by acquaintance; such knowledge is different from ordinary empirical knowledge coloured by the state of the senses and the mind.

The mind of a yogi practising concentration is disturbed, at the beginning, by many distractions, as is the surface of a lake by waves. But through persistent practice of concentration,

these distractions become attenuated. Intense concentration on
the nature of the self creates a powerful wave, which gradually
swallows up, as it were, all other waves created by past impressions. Finally, by utter non-attachment and a supreme act
of will, the last wave can be made to burst and the mind becomes free from all distractions. It acquires its natural state of
purity and reflects the true nature of the inner spirit or soul.

Raja-yoga consists of eight "limbs" or parts. The first two,
yama and niyama, denote, in a general way, self-control. The
discipline of yama includes non-injury, truthfulness, non-covet-
ousness, chastity, and non-receiving of gifts; all these bring
about purity of mind, without which spiritual contemplation is
not possible. Without self-control, the practice of yoga can injure both the yogi and others. A Sanskrit proverb says: "To
feed a cobra with milk without first taking out its poison fangs
is only to increase its venom." Niyama signifies certain habits
and observances, such as austerity, study of the scriptures, contentment, purity of body and mind, and devotion to God.

The third limb of yoga is asana, or posture. That posture
which comes easiest to the student is recommended. Different
postures are prescribed; but the general principle is to hold the
spinal column free. The yogi sits erect, holding his back, neck,
and head in a straight line, and resting the whole weight of the
upper body on the ribs. With the chest out, he finds it easy
to relax the body and think deeply.

The fourth limb is pranayama, generally called the control
of the breath. According to Hindu philosophers, the universe
consists of two primordial elements: akasa and prana, which
are the sources of matter and energy respectively. Through
their interaction all tangible objects come into existence. Prana,
which pervades the universe, is manifest in the human body in
the movement of the lungs; and this motion is related to the
breath. By controlling the breath one can gradually control

the whole physical system and even the cosmic energy. The breath is like the fly-wheel of a machine. In a large machine, first the fly-wheel moves, and then the motion is conveyed to the finer parts, until the most delicate mechanism is set in motion. The breath supplies the motive power to all parts of the body. When the breathing is regulated the whole physical system functions rhythmically. By the regulation of breathing, the yogis can perform such supernatural feats as remaining buried alive for a number of days, lying on a bed of nails, curing diseases both in themselves and in others, generating gigantic will-power, and transmitting thoughts to others. But the regulation of the breath, and the other yogic exercises, should be learnt from a competent teacher, or they will injure a man's body, nerves, and mind.

Pratyahara, the fifth limb of yoga, consists in training the mind to detach itself at will from a particular sense-organ. We retain the impression of an object only when the mind is attached to it through a sense-organ. Thus we may see, during the daytime, a thousand faces, but we remember at night only the face to which the mind felt attached. By means of pratyahara, the yogi can check the outward inclination of the mind and free it from the thraldom of the senses. The mind of the average person may be likened to a monkey which, restless by nature, has taken a deep draft of liquor, thus aggravating its restlessness, further has been stung by a scorpion, and finally has been possessed by a ghost. Just so, the naturally restless mind, after a deep dose of worldly pleasures, becomes intensely restless; it is, further, stung by jealousy, and finally possessed by the ghost of egotism. How is one to calm the excited monkey? One method is to allow it to jump about until at last it becomes tired. Likewise, the aspirant may allow the mind to move in any way it likes, himself remaining relaxed, and witness its restless movements without trying to suppress his thoughts. Whether they are good or bad, he should let them come to the surface; thus he will be able to know his inner nature, and such knowledge is, in itself, a great gain. Gradually, as the mind grows tired, the thoughts become fewer. And then the mind can be brought under control and detached from any sense-organ. Another method is to control mental restlessness by sheer power of will.

The sixth limb of yoga, dharana, consists in holding the mind *dharana* to a certain part of the body, making it feel that part alone, to the exclusion of all others. For instance, the yogi may remain aware only of the tip of his nose.

The seventh limb of yoga is called dhyana, meditation. In *dhyana* this stage the mind acquires the power to think of an object uninterruptedly. The flow of the yogi's mind to the object is unbroken, like the uninterrupted sound of a gong struck with a stick.

The eighth and last limb of yoga is called samadhi, or total *samadhi* absorption, a state of mind in which the yogi rejects the external part—the name and the form—of the object of meditation, and contemplates only its essence. He thus comes face to face with the true nature of the object, ordinarily hidden behind the outer name and form, and is no longer deceived by appearances.

The last three limbs—dharana, dhyana, and samadhi— taken together are called samyama. The mind first concentrates on an object, then continues in that state for a length of time, and lastly, by continued concentration, is able to dwell on the essence of the object. Through the application of samyama with reference to various objects, the yogi obtains supernatural powers. When by a supreme act of discrimination he rejects all the powers that come to him, regarding them as obstacles to liberation, and thus attains perfect desirelessness, the yogi achieves kaivalya or isolation. Then he realizes that

the soul, completely separate from body and mind, and untouched by time, space, and causation, is non-material. It is
pure consciousness, unchanging and immortal. The yogi who
has attained kaivalya may be compared to a ripe nut in
which the kernel is separate from the shell: he feels his soul,
detached from his body, rattling inside it, as it were. An ordinary man is like a green nut: the kernel is attached to the
shell.

According to the Samkhya philosophy, on which raja-yoga
is based, attachment to nature is the cause of the soul's bondage, and detachment from nature is liberation. Yet she is not
regarded as a man's enemy in his quest to realize the ultimate
goal; on the contrary, she is his helpmate. She has taken upon
herself, as it were, the unselfish task of assisting him, entangled
as he is in the world, to attain liberation; and with that end in
view she makes him pass through various experiences in different bodies, higher and lower. At long last, when, becoming
dissatisfied with these experiences, he isolates himself from nature and regains his lost glory, nature's task with this particular
self-forgetting soul is accomplished, and she comes to the res-
cue of another who has likewise lost his way in the trackless
wilderness of life. Thus mother nature, man's beneficent nurse,
is ceaselessly at work, guiding one lost soul after another—
through pleasure and pain, good and evil—to the haven of
peace and freedom. The Upanishads speak of the beginningless
prakriti, or nature, as consisting of three gunas, namely, sattva,
rajas, and tamas, which by their combination produce the
various physical bodies and objects of enjoyment. "One birthless soul becomes attached to prakriti for the purpose of enjoyment, when another birthless soul has left her after his
enjoyment is completed." Both the Samkhya and Yoga philos-
ophies postulate, as ultimate categories, an infinite number of

purushas, or souls, and one prakriti, or nature. The souls are conscious entities, whereas prakriti is insentient.

Patanjali asserts that through samadhi one becomes omniscient. The real source of knowledge is in the soul; the brain-cells do not create knowledge but serve as channels for its outer expression. When it is said that by destroying part of the brain the knowledge of a man can be interrupted, what is really meant is that the channels for manifesting knowledge are blocked. The purpose of study or observation is to open up the cells; the greater the number of cells functioning in the brain, the greater is the availability of a man's knowledge. While certain gross cells may be opened by means of ordinary education, certain other cells, more subtle in nature, may be made to function by means of yogic disciplines. It is said that in samadhi all the cells in the brain begin to function; thus a perfected yogi claims omniscience.

Samadhi is a superconscious state of the mind, in which ego is completely transcended. After experiencing it a man becomes a saint or a prophet. It is a higher state of mind, beyond both instinct and reason. In the realm of instinct, there is no I-consciousness, as for instance in animals, and very few mistakes are made; but the area of instinct is extremely limited. Reason functions in a wider area and is accompanied by I-consciousness. But one does not obtain certainty through reason. Furthermore, working through the data furnished by the senses, reason is incompetent to deal with the supramental experiences of God, the soul, and immortality. There is a vast area outside reason, which is the realm of superconsciousness and which can be known only by a faculty higher than reason, called intuition, inspiration, or direct and immediate perception. Through proper disciplines instinct can be transformed into reason, and reason into intuition or direct perception. All profound religious experiences are related to the area of the superconscious; it is from this that the seers and mystics draw their knowledge. The higher religions lay down disciplines for the attainment of the superconscious experience, but one can stumble upon it without going through the discipline. Generally such a person becomes dogmatic and makes fanatical claims of having found the truth. Or a person can become deranged if this exalted experience is forced upon him; just as a penniless beggar may lose his balance of mind through suddenly coming into a fortune which he has never dreamt of. A spiritual experience, like ordinary wealth, can be enjoyed to a greater degree when it has been earned by a man's own effort than when it is thrust upon him. The source of all spiritual experiences is beyond reason; reason takes a seeker of supramental truths as far as it can and then bows itself out. But although superconscious experiences are not directly obtained through reason, they must not conflict with reason. And again, when these supramental truths are presented to the world, the presentation must be couched in rational terms.

Samadhi can be attained, through proper steps, by all human beings. Each one of the steps has been reasoned out and scientifically tested.

It is said that the practice of raja-yoga becomes easy for those who are born with natural inwardness of mind and the power of concentration. But for many who are not so fortunate, and who want to practice raja-yoga, the disciplines of hatha-yoga are first recommended. The two yogas are closely connected. Hatha-yoga prepares the way for raja-yoga. As there exists a close relationship between the body and the mind, one finds it helpful and easy to control the mental states by certain physical exercises laid down in hatha-yoga. For the practice of hatha-yoga, a qualified teacher is absolutely necessary.

Two major disciplines of hatha-yoga are posture and control of the breath. Eighty-four postures are prescribed; these make the body firm, light, and free from disease, and also help in the practice of concentration, the suppression of carnal desire, and the correction of the humours of the body. Next comes control of the breath. It is a matter of common observance that there is a close relationship between the breath and the mind: when the breathing is irregular, the mind wanders, and when the breathing is controlled, the mind is calmer. One invites serious physical malady through incorrect practice of breath-control. The teachers of this yoga also speak of various other exercises for the inner cleansing of the body. The main purpose of hatha-yoga is to increase the strength, vitality, and digestive power, as well as to remove various physical ailments. A healthy body and long life are important factors in the realization of the spiritual goal in the present life.

It appears from a study of the religious history of India that at different times different types of spiritual experience have been emphasized. Thus, for instance, happiness in heaven was prized during the early Vedic period, the realization of the non-dual Brahman—through Vedantic disciplines—at the time of the Upanishads, and communion with the Personal God—through love—at the time of the Puranas. This is, of course, a very general statement. During the nineteenth century Ramakrishna and his great disciple Vivekananda laid special emphasis on the manifestation of God in man. Ramakrishna experienced the highest fruit of all the yogas and communed with God in various ways. But in the end he said that the manifestation of God in man appealed to him most. He asked his disciples to serve men as visible images of God and to alleviate their misery; but he derided the idea of showing them pity. One day the young Vivekananda prayed to Ramakrishna for the boon that he might commune with God in samadhi for several days at a time, opening his eyes once in a while to take a little physical nourishment. Ramakrishna reproached him and said: "Why are you so eager to see God with eyes closed? Can't you see Him with eyes open?" He explained that the presence of God was felt not only when one shut the eyes; God could also be seen when one looked around. Service to the hungry, sick, and ignorant in the proper spirit was as effective as any other spiritual discipline. For several days before his passing away, Ramakrishna instructed the disciple as to how to minister to the spiritual needs of humanity. He also said many times that he himself would be willing to come back to earth even as a dog if given the privilege of serving others.

After the passing away of his master, Vivekananda practised intense austerities, following the time-honoured disciplines of the monastic life, and several times resolved to end his days in meditation in a mountain cave; but each time he was thrown out, as it were, by an unseen power. At last he discovered that one of his missions was to serve the Indian masses by removing their poverty, sickness, and ignorance. He came to America to explore the possibilities of applying scientific and technological knowledge to achieve that purpose. Another mission was to serve Western men and women by bringing to them the message of Vedanta in order to deepen their spiritual consciousness and their religious outlook. Later he established the Ramakrishna Order of monks, whose members take the two vows of personal liberation and service to humanity. The spiritual discipline of the monks of the Order alternates between worship and service. At the conclusion of his poem "To a Friend" the Swami wrote:

> Thy God is here before thee now,
> Revealed in all these myriad forms:

> Rejecting them, where seekest thou
> His presence? He who freely shares
> His love with every living thing
> Proffers true service unto God.

Before his death Vivekananda said: "May I be born again and again and suffer thousands of miseries, so that I may worship the only God that exists and the only God that I believe in: the sum total of all souls."

IX.

Tantra: A Way of Realization

MODERN research demonstrates the close affinity of the Tantra system of religious philosophy to the Vedas; Tantra itself speaks of its Vedic origin. In its subsequent development it shows the influence of the Upanishads, Yoga, and the Puranas. The ritualistic worship of modern Hinduism has been greatly coloured by it, and this fact is particularly noticeable in Bengal, Kashmir, Gujarat, and Malabar.

Reality, according to Tantra, is chit, or pure consciousness, which is identical with sat, or being, and ananda, or bliss. Thus both Vedanta and Tantra show a general agreement about the nature of reality, with, however, an important difference which will be presently stated. This being-consciousness-bliss, or Satchidananda, becomes restricted through maya, and its transcendental nature is then expressed in terms of forms and categories.

According to the Vedas, as already stated, Satchidananda, or Brahman, is in its true nature pure spirit; and maya, which is inherent in it, functions only on the relative plane at the time of creation, preservation, and destruction; neither is the creation ultimately real, nor are created beings, for true knowledge reveals only an undifferentiated consciousness. According to Tantra, on the other hand, Satchidananda is called Siva-Sakti, the hyphenated word suggesting that Siva, or the Absolute, and Sakti, or its creative power, are eternally conjoined like a word and its meaning: the one cannot be thought of without the other. A conception of pure consciousness or being which denies Sakti, or the power to become, is, according to Tantra, only half of the truth. Satchidananda is essentially endowed with the power of self-evolution and self-involution. Therefore perfect experience is the experience of the whole— that is to say, of consciousness as being and consciousness as power to become. It is only in the relative world that Siva and Sakti are thought of as separate entities. Furthermore, Tantra affirms that both the world process and the jiva, or soul, are real, and not merely illusory superimpositions upon Brahman. In declaring that the jiva finally becomes one with the reality, Tantra differs from qualified non-dualism and pure dualism.

Maya, according to Tantra, veils reality and polarizes it into what is conscious and what is unconscious, what is existent and what is non-existent, what is pleasant and what is unpleasant. Through polarization, the infinite becomes finite, the undifferentiated differentiated, the immeasurable measured. For the same reason, non-dual reality becomes evolved—and this becoming is real and not merely apparent as in Vedanta— into a multiplicity of correlated "centres" or entities of diverse nature, acting and reacting upon one another in various ways. Some of the centres, such as human beings, evolve the power of feeling, cognition, and will, while others lack such power, there being various degrees of power or lack of power. Some centres, again, are knowers, and some, objects of knowledge; some, enjoyers, and some, objects of enjoyment. The various determining conditions which constitute and maintain a centre, for instance, a jiva, also limit or restrict it, accounting for its actions and reactions. These determinants are the "fetters" (pasa) which weave the whole fabric of the jiva's phenomenal life. By them it is bound and made to act like an "animal" (pasu).

Though reality evolves, by its own inscrutable power, into a multiplicity of centres animate and inanimate, yet in its true nature it always remains pure consciousness, being, and bliss. In the state of evolution, reality does not cease to be itself, though neither the act nor the fact of evolution is denied by Tantra.

Thus a finite centre in any position in the "curve" of evolution never ceases to be a "point" of pure reality through which the infinite opens itself and through which it can be reached. When a jiva faces this point it is none other than reality, and when it turns away from the point and faces the veil of maya it is finite, conditioned, and bound by fetters. Thus in every jiva-centre there are elements of both individuality and infinitude, phenomenality and reality. One direction of the functioning of maya, called the "outgoing current," creates the jiva-centre with its fetters; a reversal of this direction, called the "return current," reveals the infinite. Tantra (especially its disciplines prescribed in the "left-hand" path, to be explained later) shows the way to change the outgoing current into the return current, transforming what operates as a bond for the jiva into a "releaser" or "liberator." As Tantra says: "One must rise by that by which one falls"; "the very poison that kills becomes the elixir of life when used by the wise." The various impulses and desires associated with the outgoing current form, as it were, the net of the phenomenal world in which the jiva has been caught. Some of these impulses appear to be cardinal or primary knots in this net. The only question is how to transform these cardinal impulses for material enjoyment (bhoga) into spiritual experiences (yoga): how to bring about the sublimation of desires. If this can be done, what now binds will be reversed in its working, and the finite jiva will realize its identity with infinite reality.

The jiva, caught in the outgoing current, perceives duality and cherishes the notions of pleasure and pain, acceptance and rejection, body and soul, spirit and matter, and so on. But if the non-duality of Siva-Sakti alone exists, as asserted by Tantra, all these distinctions must be relative. Thus the distinction between man and woman, the desire for each other which is one of the cardinal desires, and the physical union between them all belong to the relative plane, where a perennial conflict between the flesh and the spirit is assumed, and where a jiva acts like an animal bound by the fetters of common convention. The distinction is a valid one and may even be valuable as long as the jiva remains on the relative plane. The observance of moral or social conventions, however desirable on that plane, does not make the jiva other than an animal. In order that the jiva may know that it is really Siva (the Absolute), it must resolve every kind of duality and realize the fact that whatever exists and functions on the physical or moral level is Siva-Sakti, the ever inseparable reality and its power. When one realizes that the whole process of creation, preservation, and destruction is but the manifestation of the lila, or sportive pleasure, of Siva-Sakti, one does not see anything carnal or gross in the universe; for such a one everything becomes an expression of Siva-Sakti. The special technique of the Tantric discipline is to transform the outgoing current of diversification into the return current of gradual integration, to gather separation, polarity, and even opposition into identification, harmony, and peace.

The two currents, however, do not operate singly, one excluding the other; they are concurrent, though the emphasis, which oscillates, is now laid on one and now on the other. Thus in all affirmations of duality and difference, the affirmation of non-duality and identity is immanent, and one sees unities, equalities, and similarities, and not a mere chaos of colliding particles, even when the outgoing current functions in the creation and preservation of the universe. Our ordinary experience, too, shows system, though this system reveals to us limited and conditioned identities. In brief, though differentiation is the prevailing feature of the outgoing current, identity is either implicit in it, or conditionally visible.

Let us take the example of a man and woman. Subject to certain limits and conditions, the two in a way can be equated; the difference between them is patent but can be eliminated. Emphasis on the difference, however, constitutes the fetters of man and woman, as is seen in common experience. These fetters will disappear when their real identity and not their pragmatic equality is realized. Hence the question is how to affirm or rather reaffirm an identity which is veiled.

The method of non-dualistic Vedanta is to negate all limiting adjuncts, which it calls unreal, until one sees nothing but Brahman, or pure and undifferentiated consciousness, in the man and woman. In order to reach the affirmation of oneness, every vestige of duality must be rigorously discarded; in other words, Vedanta asks the aspirants to renounce the world of names and forms. But this is more easily said than done, for such renunciation can be practised only by a few.

Tantra, whose technique is different, prescribes the discipline of sublimation. Physical man and woman, floating along the outgoing current of the cosmic process, are, no doubt, different from each other, but by means of the return current they can be sublimated into cosmic principles and realized as the one whole, that is, Siva-Sakti. In reversing the outgoing current, the aspirant has to "bring together" the complements or poles so as to realize their identity; thus the physical union of man and woman is sublimated into the creative union of

Siva-Sakti. The left-hand path of Tantra under certain very stringent conditions prescribes to the aspirant, or sadhaka, belonging to the "heroic" type to be described later, spiritual disciplines of ritualistic readjustment with woman, and shows how to sublimate the so-called "carnal" act gradually until the experience of the supreme non-dual Siva-Sakti with its perfect bliss is attained. The technique is to make the very same carnal desire which constitutes the strongest fetter of the animal man an "opening" or channel for the experience of Satchidananda. If the right track is followed and all the conditions are fulfilled, the aspirant succeeds in his endeavour.

The Tantric method of sublimation consists of three steps: purification, elevation, and reaffirmation of identity on the plane of pure consciousness. First, the aspirant must rid himself of the dross of grossness by reversing the outgoing current into the return current. According to Tantra, in the process of evolution, the pure cosmic principles (tattvas) at a certain stage cross the line and pass into impure principles, the latter constituting the realm of nature, which is like a "coiled" curve, in which the jiva is held a prisoner and where it wanders, caught in a net of natural determinism from which there is no escape unless the coiled curve can be made to uncoil itself and open a channel for its release and ascent into the realm of the pure cosmic principles. Until this is done the jiva remains afloat on the outgoing current, moves with it, and cherishes desires which are gross or carnal. Whether yielding pleasure or pain, these desires fasten the chain upon the jiva with additional links. Its hope lies in uncoiling the coil of nature that has closed upon it. This is called in the technical language of Tantra the "awakening" of the Kundalini, or coiled-up serpent power, by which one moves from the plane of impure principles to that of pure principles. The head of this coiled serpent is turned downward; it must be turned upward. This change of the direction of the serpent power, which after evolving the jiva remains involved in it, is called purification. The next step is called elevation: the order in which the cosmic principles move along the outgoing current must be reversed with the starting of the return current. Ascent is to be made in the reverse order to that in which the descent was made. The aspirant must raise himself from the grosser and more limited elements to the subtler and more general ones until he attains to the realization of Siva-Sakti. The last step is the reaffirmation in consciousness of his identity with Siva-Sakti. This is the general framework of the method of sublimation into which can be fitted all the methods of sublimation followed by the dualistic, non-dualistic, and other systems of thought.

The spiritual awakening of a sadhaka is described in Tantra by means of the symbol of the awakening and rising of the Kundalini power. What is this Kundalini? Properly understood, it is not something mystical or esoteric, peculiar to Tantra, but the basis of the spiritual experiences described by all religious faiths. Every genuine spiritual experience, such as the seeing of light or a vision, or communion with the Deity, is only a manifestation of the ascent of the Kundalini. Let us try to understand the Kundalini with the help of an illustration from classical physics. There are two kinds of energy associated with a piece of matter: potential and kinetic, the sum-total of which is a constant. The kinetic energy, which may be only a fraction of the total energy, is involved in the movement or action of a body. According to Tantra, the Kundalini, in the form of cosmic energy, is present in everything, even in a particle of matter. Only a fraction of it, like the kinetic energy, is operative, while an unmeasured residuum is left, like the potential energy, "coiled up" and untapped at the "base root." It is a vast magazine of power, of which the operative energy, like the kinetic energy of the particle, is only a fraction. In the jiva-centre, also, are both this potential energy of the Kundalini, which is the storehouse of the energy of the body (physical, subtle, and causal), and also the active energy of the Kundalini, which accounts for the action and movement of the jiva. The coiled-up Kundalini is the central pivot upon which the whole complex apparatus of the body and mind moves and turns. A specific ratio between the active and total energies of the Kundalini determines the present condition and behaviour of the bodily apparatus. A change in the ratio is necessary to effect a change in its present working efficiency by transforming the grosser bodily elements into finer. A transformation, dynamization, and sublimation of the physical, mental, and vital apparatus is only possible through what is called the rousing of the Kundalini and its reorientation from "downward facing" to "upward facing." By the former the physical body has been made a "coiled curve," limited in character, restricted in functions and possibilities. By the force of the latter it breaks its fetters and transcends its limitations. This is the general principle. But there are various forms of spiritual discipline by which this magazine of latent power can be acted upon. Faith and love act as a most powerful lever to raise the coiled-up Kundalini; so also the disciplines of raja-yoga and jnana-yoga. The repetition of the Lord's name or a holy mantra, and even music, help in this process. Tantra recognizes all this. The student of Tantra should bear in mind the psychological aspect of the process of the ascent of the Kundalini, which is more of an unfoldment, expansion, and elevation of consciousness than a mechanical accession to an increased and higher power. The aim of waking the Kundalini is not the acquisition of greater power for the purpose of performing miraculous feats or the enjoyment of material pleasures; it is the realization of Satchidananda.

The passage of the awakened Kundalini lies through the Sushumna, which is described as the central nerve in the nervous system. A kind of hollow canal, the Sushumna passes through the spinal column connecting the base centre (chakra) at the bottom of the spine with the centre at the cerebrum. Tantra speaks of six centres through which Sushumna passes; these centres are so many spheres or planes, described in Tantra as different-coloured lotuses with varying numbers of petals. In the ordinary worldly person these centres are closed, and the lotuses droop down like buds. As the Kundalini rises through the Sushumna canal and touches the centres, these buds turn upward as fully opened flowers and the aspirant obtains spiritual experiences. The goal in spiritual practice is to make the Kundalini ascend from the centres which are lower and more veiled to those which are higher and more conscious. During this upward journey of the Kundalini, the jiva is not quite released from the relative state till it reaches the sixth centre or plane, which is the "opening" for pure and perfect experience. At this sixth centre (the two-petalled white lotus located at the junction of the eyebrows) the jiva sheds its ego and burns the seed of duality, and its higher self rises from the ashes of its lower self. It now dies physically, as it were, in order to be able to live in pure consciousness. The sixth centre is the key by which the power in the thousand-petalled lotus in the cerebrum, which is like the limitless ocean, is switched on to the little reservoir which is the individual self, filling the latter and making it overflow and cease to be the little reservoir. Finally the Kundalini rises to the lotus at the cerebrum and becomes united with Siva, or the Absolute, and the aspirant realizes, in a transcendental experience, his union with Siva-Sakti. The opening of the petals of the thousand-petalled lotus, which endows the illumined person with omniscience, is equivalent to the functioning of all the brain cells of a yogi in samadhi, as described in the preceding chapter.

Tantra discusses the qualifications of the teacher and the student, and also mantras or sacred words, diagrams, deities, rituals, and mental dispositions, all of which are important in the practice of its disciplines.

A qualified teacher, or guru, must be a man of good birth and unsullied character. Compassionate and serene, he should be versed in the Tantric and other scriptures, repeat regularly God's holy name, and offer oblations in the sacrificial fire. Furthermore, he should possess a pleasing disposition and the power to fulfil his disciples' wishes. The help of a guru is indispensable for a student of Tantra. Vital changes take place in him as the Kundalini ascends and the impure elements of his body and mind become pure. In the practice of spiritual disciplines, the aspirant passes through a series of crises and needs outside help. It is true that the Divine Mother, who is none other than the Kundalini itself, bestows this help in the form of grace whenever a real crisis comes, but a human medium is necessary. The guru is an adept in the Tantric practices, has experimented with its disciplines, and has verified their result for himself. The disciple does not look upon his guru as a physical being, but as the embodiment of God. As the physician of the soul, the guru occupies a position of extreme responsibility, guides the disciple in difficult practices, and looks after his welfare in every respect.

Like the teacher, the disciple should come of a good family and possess a blameless character and guileless nature. Keen-minded, versed in the scriptures, and kind-hearted, he should have faith in the life after death, perform his duties toward his parents, and be free from pride of lineage, scholarship, or wealth. Furthermore, he should shun the company of nonbelievers and be ready to serve the teacher in all humility. The three types of aspirants will be described later.

A responsible teacher should not be in a hurry to give initiation nor should an aspirant accept as his teacher a person to whom he is not attracted. The mode of initiation varies, depending upon the competence of the teacher and the qualifications of the student. An ordinary initiation is given by means of elaborate rituals. But these become secondary in the higher type of initiation through which the disciple very soon becomes blessed with deep spiritual experiences.

Mantras play a most important part in the Tantric discipline, just as sacrifices and hymns in the disciplines of the Vedas and the Puranas respectively. The word *mantra* means, literally, "that which, when reflected upon, gives liberation." The mantra is the sound-equivalent of the Deity, that is to say, chit or consciousness; the external image is the material form of the mantra. The sound-vibration is the first manifestation of chit and nearest to it. It is really intermediate between pure consciousness and the physical object, being neither absolutely immaterial like the former nor dense like the latter. Tantra regards vibration as a manifestation of the cosmic energy, or Sakti, and teaches that as such it can lead to the realization of chit, which otherwise eludes the grasp of even an intelligent person. Thus mantras are not mere words, but are forms of concentrated thought of exceeding potency; they are revealed to the seers in the hour of their illumination. The aspirant finds that a mantra and the deity with which it is associated are identical, the deity being the illumination embodied in the mantra. To the ignorant, the vibration created by the mantra is only a physical phenomenon, and the mantra itself nothing but a sound, but to the adept it is both illuminative and creative. Illumination is hidden in the mantra, like a tree in a seed. As soon as this illumination is expressed, the mantra becomes endowed with a wonderful power and reveals the cosmic energy latent in it. Tantra believes that some of the basic mantras have not been created by human brains, but are eternally existent, and that through their repetition the aspirant attains to perfection.

Mystical diagrams called "yantras" are used in the Tantric rituals. A yantra is a diagrammatic equivalent of the deity, just as a mantra is its sound-equivalent. It is not like the schematic sketch of a molecule, used by the chemist, but is a full representation, as revealed to the adept, of the basic power which evolves and maintains an object of worship. When the yantra is given real potency, the Deity is there. In the Tantric ritual the yantra is the object of worship, the image being its tangible representation. There is a fundamental relationship between the mantra and the yantra.

The image of the Deity through which one communes with ultimate reality is also an embodiment of consciousness and not just a figure of wood or stone. If the worship is properly performed, then the image, the mantra, the yantra, and the various other accessories of worship all become changed into forms and expressions of consciousness, as in the Christian communion the wine and bread into the blood and flesh of Christ.

To the uninitiated, the mantras and the yantras employed in Tantric worship may appear as meaningless jargon and magical diagrams. The same is true, as far as the uninformed are concerned, of all the cumbrous formulas, equations, and notations used by the chemist and the physicist. For example, $E=mc^2$ makes no more sense to the ignorant than a mantra, for instance, Om or Hring. The same is true of the mystical formulas used in Tantra; they are really shorthand statements of certain basic experiences. The same faithful exactitude in the ritual is demanded of the student of Tantra, and the same degree of proficiency in the understanding of mantras and yantras, as is required of the student in the physical sciences. A popular version of the Kundalini or the other principles of Tantra may be given, just as one may also be given of the Relativity Theory or quantum mechanics; but the actual proofs lie, in the one case as in the other, in delicate experiments which are unfortunately beyond the reach and comprehension of the average individual. Tantra insists that mantras are efficacious, that the diagrams used in the worship are potent, that the deities, or devatas, are conscious entities, that supernatural powers are attained, and that the earnest aspirant experiences the rise of the Kundalini through the different spinal centres and finally realizes his identity with Satchidananda.

Let us briefly consider a Tantric ritual as observed in the worship. The aim of Tantra is to guide aspirants to realize both the supreme end of liberation and the secondary ends of wealth, sense-pleasure, and righteousness, according to their inner evolution and desires. It therefore lays down an endless variety of rituals suited to different times, places, and individual competencies. Usually a Tantric ritual consists in the assigning of the different parts of the body to different deities, the purifying of the elements of the body, breath-control, meditation, imparting of life to the image, and mental and physical worship. These are all calculated to transform the worshipper, the worshipped, the accessories, and the act of worship into consciousness, which they all are in essence. As the culmination of the ritual, the aspirant realizes his oneness with all. Harmony on the physical and mental planes are necessary for success in worship; this is created in the gross physical elements by means of prescribed postures, in the vital breaths by means of breath-control, in the cerebrum by the correct utterance of mantras, and in the mental states by meditation,

TANTRA: A WAY OF REALIZATION   159

Ablution (snana) purifies the physical body, and this purification is followed by an inner satisfaction (tarpana). By means of
appropriate meditative rituals the gross, subtle, and causal
bodies are freed of their respective taints (bhutasuddhi). The
purpose of meditation (dhyana) is to enable the worshipper to
feel his oneness with the Deity. This meditation on oneness, the
central feature of the Tantric worship, is quite different from
that of dualistic religions, which maintain a distinction between the Deity and the devotee. "Only by becoming divine
can one worship the divine." The last part of the ritual consists
of a sacrifice (homa) in which the devotee completely sur-
renders himself to the Deity, merges in him, and loses his
identity in him. At this stage there is no more distinction between the worshipper and the worshipped, the finite and the
infinite, the individual and the Absolute.

It is claimed that Tantra is a kind of experimental science
and that the realization promised by it is an experimentally
verified fact. Theories and speculations are tentative only; the
motto of Tantra is "Live by what you can actually prove and
verify." Nothing need be accepted on the basis of such a
statement as "Thus saith the Lord." But initially it is required
of the sadhaka, as in all the sciences, to follow the guidance of
a teacher who has tried the experiment before him and seen
the result for himself.

Several paths have been prescribed by Tantra for the awakening of the Kundalini; one of these is called the Vamachara
or "left-hand" path, which, partly on account of ignorance of
the principles involved and partly on account of its abuse by
irresponsible persons, has made the whole science of Tantra
suspect. The ritual of this path is, like other genuine spiritual
practices, based upon the principle of the "return current,"
which seeks to reverse the process that creates the bonds of the
animal man. The five ingredients used by followers of this path

are cereals, fish, meat, wine, and sexual union. These, however, have different connotations for different classes of aspirants. The underlying principle of Vamachara is to emphasize the fact that a man makes progress in spiritual life not by cowardly and falsely shunning that which makes him fall, but by seizing upon it and sublimating it so as to make it a means of liberation. For a certain type of aspirant, called "heroic," the actual drinking of wine and practice of sexual union are prescribed, and the teacher carefully points out that the joy and stimulation arising from these are to be utilized for the uplift of the mind from the physical plane. For instance, the aspirant is asked first to offer wine to the Deity and then to partake of it as a sacramental offering. The same is the case with cereals, fish, and meat. The pleasure resulting from their enjoyment is gradually sublimated. Sexual union, the disciple is taught, is something sacred, whose purpose is the creation of new life, and it should therefore not be resorted to in an irresponsible manner. Tantra never countenances sexual excess or irregularity for the purpose of the gratification of carnal desire. To break chastity, it says, is to lose or shorten life. Furthermore, sexual union has a deeper spiritual significance in that it reveals behind duality a unity which is present in all phenomenal experiences. Even on the physical plane, a couple becomes united in the sexual act, but the unity of Siva-Sakti and the bliss derived from it are experienced only by liberated souls. Woman, associated with the Tantric practices in order to help man in his path of renunciation, is an object of veneration to all schools of Tantra. She is regarded as the embodiment of Sakti, or the power that projects and pervades the universe. To insult a woman is a grievous sin. The aspirant learns from the teacher how to use the aforesaid five ingredients for his spiritual awakening. By the power of the mantra, the rituals, meditation, prayer, sincerity, and the grace of the guru and the

Divine Mother, the disciple gradually develops an understanding by which everything he does in his ordinary life becomes an act of worship and which makes him realize what Sankaracharya meant when he wrote in one of his hymns to the primordial Sakti: "O Lady Supreme, may all the functions of my mind be Thy remembrance; may all my words be Thy praise; may all my acts be an obeisance to Thee!"

Tantra divides sadhakas, or spiritual aspirants, into three groups according to their mental disposition: animal, heroic, and divine. The man with animal disposition (pasu) moves along the outgoing current and earns merit and demerit from his worldly activities. He has not yet raised himself above the common round of convention, nor has he cut the three knots of "hate, fear, and shame." Swayed by his passions, he is a slave of six hostile impulses: lust, greed, pride, anger, delusion, and envy. He is not allowed even to touch the five ingredients of the left-hand ritual.

The student competent for the hazardous ritual with the five ingredients already described is called a hero (vira). He has the inner strength to "play with fire" and to burn his worldly bonds with it. Established in complete self-control, he does not forget himself even in the most trying and tempting circumstances. He is a man of fearless disposition, inspiring terror in those who cherish animal propensities. Pure in motive, gentle in speech, strong in body, resourceful, courageous, intelligent, adventurous, and humble, he cherishes only what is good.

The sadhaka of divine (divya) disposition has risen above all the bonds of desire and has nothing to sublimate. One of the Tantric scriptures describes such an aspirant as sparing in speech, beloved of all, introspective, steady, sagacious, and solicitous about others' welfare. He never swerves from the path of truth and can do no evil. Good in every way, he is regarded as the embodiment of Siva. In his worship he does not need physical aids for rousing his spiritual emotions; the meditative mood is spontaneous with him. He is always in ecstasy, enjoying "inner woman and wine." For the five ingredients used by a hero he substitutes consciousness (chit), bliss (ananda), and exaltation (bhava).

Tantra claims that its disciplines have a universal application; it admits the validity of the rituals of the Vedas, the discrimination and renunciation of the Upanishads, the purifying disciplines of raja-yoga, and the passionate love for the Deity described in the Puranas. It exhorts the sadhaka to exercise will and self-effort, practise self-surrender, and supplicate for divine grace. Tantra promises its devotees not only enjoyment of worldly happiness but also liberation, and acknowledges that the power of the Kundalini can be aroused by the sincere pursuit of the spiritual disciplines recommended by all the great religions of the world.

Ramakrishna, in modern times, followed the disciplines of Tantra and demonstrated them to be a valid way of realization. Under the guidance of a woman teacher he practised the rituals of all the various Tantric schools, achieving in three days the result promised by each of them. The goddess Kali, one of the forms of the Divine Sakti, was his chosen ideal. Born with a spiritual disposition, he had no need of the five ingredients of the Tantric worship in their physical form. As he uttered the name of Kali, he would be filled with the joy of divine inebriation, and people actually saw him in that state reeling or talking incoherently like a drunkard. After the observance of a few preliminary rites, he often entered into deep samadhi and was overwhelmed by a spiritual fervour. Evil ceased to exist for him, and the word *carnal* lost all meaning. He went into ecstasy at the sight of a prostitute, of drunkards revelling in a tavern, and of the sexual union of a dog and bitch. The whole world was revealed to him as the play of Siva-Sakti, and he beheld everywhere the power and beauty of the Divine Mother. He did not, like a Vedantic scholar, repudiate the world as maya, but gave it a spiritual status, seeing in it the manifestation of chit and ananda. Ramakrishna's biography narrates many of his experiences derived from the Tantric practices. The barrier between matter and energy broke down for him, and he actually saw even a grain of sand and a blade of grass vibrating with energy. The universe appeared to him as a lake of mercury or of silver, and he had a vision of the ultimate cause of the universe as a huge luminous triangle giving birth every moment to an infinite number of universes. He acquired the various supernatural powers of yoga, which make a man almost omnipotent, and he spurned them all as of no spiritual value. In a vision of maya he saw a pregnant woman of exquisite beauty emerging from the waters of the Ganges. Presently she came to the land and gave birth to a child, whom she began to nurse tenderly. A moment later she assumed a terrible aspect, seized the child between her grim jaws, and crushed it; as she swallowed the child, she re-entered the waters of the Ganges. Ramakrishna directly perceived the ascent of the Kundalini, and later described to his disciples its various movements: fishlike, birdlike, monkeylike, and so on. One of the results of his practice of Tantra was the deepening of his respect for womanhood. To him every woman was the embodiment of the Divine Sakti, and he could not, even in a dream, regard a woman in any other way. His relationship with his own wife was entirely on the spiritual plane. He taught that the most effective way for a man to overcome carnal desire was to regard woman as the manifestation of the Divine Mother. He forbade his disciples, however, to practise the rituals prescribed for a sadhaka of heroic disposition.

X.

Hinduism in Practice

WE HAVE thus far been discussing mainly the philosophical aspects of Hinduism. But the religion practised in daily life by the average Hindu is, to all outward appearances, different from what is taught in the Upanishads and the Bhagavad Gita. It is associated with worship of images and with symbols, music, dancing, processions, prayer, feasting, fasting, and so on. Popular religion everywhere is dualistic; the object of worship is the Personal God, or one of His manifestations, who is propitiated by various rituals.

Let us try to understand the Vedantic concept of the Personal God. Vedanta, as we have seen, includes dualism, qualified non-dualism, and absolute non-dualism. Dualism anthropomorphizes ultimate reality and regards it as the Personal God who creates, preserves, and destroys the universe, while remaining outside it. It is by His grace that a man attains to liberation.

According to qualified non-dualism, reality, called Vishnu or the all-pervading spirit, is present everywhere in the creation and represents the totality of individual bodies, minds, and souls. But at the same time, as the Personal God, He dwells in His special heaven. This may be explained by the illustration of a man, who is endowed not only with a body and innumerable living cells, but with a soul besides. Though the soul functions in every part of the body, yet its presence is especially felt in the heart, just as the owner of a large house may occupy any part of it, but there is a special room where he is usually found. Reality, or God, includes both the physical universe and living souls: the totality of physical bodies is His body, all souls are His living cells, and His own soul or essence is the Personal God. A man can lose a limb, or a number of living cells, and still live; likewise, nothing happens to God if part of the physical world or a number of living beings are destroyed. Thus, according to qualified non-dualism, God is one and without a second, though His non-duality admits of distinctions. His personal aspect, whose grace it is that liberates the soul, is worshipped by the devotees.

According to absolute non-dualism, pure consciousness appears, through maya, as the conditioned Brahman, and assumes different forms and names for the welfare of devotees in the phenomenal world. Each of these forms—Vishnu, or the Father in heaven, or Jehovah, or Allah—is regarded by its respective devotees as the Personal God. Form and formlessness, as Ramakrishna said, are manifestations of one and the same Reality. By worshipping the Personal God with rituals and devotion, a devotee can attain the knowledge of the Impersonal Absolute if he so desires. Sankaracharya instituted in his monasteries the worship of Sakti or the feminine aspect of reality; Ramakrishna, at the beginning of his spiritual disciplines, worshipped Kali and ultimately realized Brahman. Love of God leads to the knowledge of Brahman.

The deities of popular Hinduism are symbols of the Personal God. Their images are seen in the temples and shrines. A popular saying in India speaks of three hundred million and thirty-three thousand deities worshipped by three hundred million people. Yet the Hindu religion is essentially monotheistic. Whatever deity or aspect of reality is worshipped is, to his devotee, the supreme God, other deities being only parts of Him. Therefore the monotheism of the Hindus does not exclude other gods; it includes them all. An Upanishad says: "Rudra is truly one, for the knowers of Brahman do not admit the existence of a second. He alone rules all the worlds by His powers. He dwells as the inner Self of every living being. After having created all the worlds, He, their Protector, takes them back unto Himself at the end of time." The word *Rudra* in the text denotes the Impersonal Absolute. Later, in the Puranas, it becomes Siva, who is the personification of Brahman in His destructive aspect. Again in the same Upanishad one reads: "He, the omniscient Rudra, the creator of the gods and the bestower of their powers, the support of the universe, He who in the beginning gave birth to the conditioned Brahman —may He endow us with clear intellect." All the Upanishads proclaim the non-duality of the Godhead.

A deity can be worshipped for two purposes: either for the fulfilment of worldly desires or for ultimate deliverance from the bondage of the world. Some devotees, conscious of their inability to contemplate their identity with the supreme spirit, pursue a concrete form of worship as a spiritual discipline and cherish the hope of ultimately giving up dualistic thought. Thus they are led from the Personal God to impersonal reality, from ritual to contemplation, from audible prayer to the experience of inner peace and silence. Other worshippers, however, like to preserve the distinction between God and themselves and enjoy the bliss of divine communion in various ways.

Popular worship in India is generally pervaded by a spirit of joyousness and merriment. The atmosphere of the temple is not gloomy or heavy, but reverberates with songs, hymns, and shouts of mirth. This is mainly due to the fact that a Hindu really feels in the shrine the presence of the deity, who is the embodiment of bliss. There is also the firm conviction that God never forsakes His devotees, however wicked they may be, if they approach Him with devotion and contrite hearts. "He carries, for those who are always devoted to Him, what they lack and preserves for them what they already have." "Even if the worst sinner worships Me with singleness of mind, he should be regarded as a saint because his efforts are whole-hearted. Quickly he realizes the soul of religion and enjoys eternal peace. I promise that My devotee never meets with destruction." A Hindu mystic sang about the compassion of the Divine Mother: "There may be wicked children, but never a wicked Mother." A devotee at moments of distress gets relief by thinking that he has the Divine Mother to protect him. But underlying all prayer and worship there is the sincere desire for deliverance from the suffering of repeated births and deaths in the phenomenal world.

According to a popular saying, a Hindu celebrates "thirteen holy days in twelve months." These are occasions for festivities accompanied by congregational singing, pilgrimages, baths in sacred waters, and visits to temples. They afford a relief from the dreary tasks of the daily life of the world. Thus one finds even today a surprising amount of contentment among the Indian masses in spite of their lack of material comforts; they are free from the worries and tension which plague the life of the people in a secular society.

The popular worship of modern times, which has its source in the rituals of the Vedas, emphasizes bhakti or love of God, and also faith rather than reason. The seed of bhakti was sown in the ritualistic portion of the Vedas and was developed, later, in the Agamas and the Puranas. There has been a continuity in religious thought from the earliest Vedic period to the present time, though its outer expression has considerably changed. Therefore a brief discussion of the Vedic rituals will enable the reader to understand the Hindu view of ritualistic worship and its bearing upon the attainment of man's highest goal.

Various sacrifices, which consist of offering oblations for the propitiation of the deities, have been dealt with throughout the four sections of the Vedas. The Mantra section contains hymns and prayers used in the sacrifices. The Brahmana section gives the rules for the sacrifices, deals with their accessories, and also reveals the abstruse meaning of the mantras or sacred formulas. The Aranyaka portion lays down symbolic sacrifice and also the various meditations to be used as substitutes for the accessories of a tangible sacrifice, when such accessories are not available. The Upanishads deal with the knowledge of Brahman, but recognize the place of ritualistic meditation at certain stages of spiritual development.

One of the six systems of Indian philosophy, namely the Purva-Mimamsa, regards the performance of sacrifices as the sole injunction of the Vedas; through it the worshipper enjoys prosperity in this world, and happiness in heaven. The utilitarian aspect of sacrifices is based upon the Hindu belief in the interdependence of gods and men. The Bhagavad Gita says that Brahma created men and asked them to regard sacrifice as the "cow of plenty." The gods and men should cherish one another. "For, cherished by sacrifices, the gods will bestow upon you the pleasures you desire. He is verily a thief who enjoys the things they give without giving them anything in return." This reciprocity is the basis of Vedic sacrifices; the beneficent gods had to be pleased if one was to secure boons from them, and the maleficent deities had to be appeased to ward off any harm. The essence of sacrifice is to offer to the deities the things one greatly values; the offering should be accompanied by sincerity and faith. The deities that people sought to propitiate in Vedic times were, among others, Indra, Mitra, Varuna, and Agni. Agni, the fire-god, became important among the deities because the oblations were offered in the fire, which came to be regarded as the mediator between gods and men. But it should always be remembered that the deities and rituals are valid only in the phenomenal world.

The Vedas speak of various rites, some of which are optional, some obligatory, some to be performed on special occasions, and some in the form of penances to expiate the sins of the past. The optional rites are meant for those who cherish desires, for instance, for a son or an empire; they may or may not be performed, depending upon the wishes of the agent. The obligatory rites, such as daily religious devotions, do not bring about any specific result, but their non-performance produces harm. Their indirect result is the purification of the mind and the development of introspection. The rites to be performed on special occasions have a deep religious significance and tend to spiritualize the important events of life from birth to death. Some of the important occasions are when a man is born, when he is given a name, when he is first fed with solid food, when he is invested with the sacred thread enabling him to study the Vedas, when he marries, and when he is cremated. The investiture with the sacred thread, or initiation ceremony, which marks his spiritual birth, is the most important event in a man's life. By means of expiatory rites past sins are forgiven, and an aspirant is thus enabled to practise his spiritual disciplines with a somewhat contented mind.

Now we shall discuss the place given to rituals in the Upanishads. The goal of the Upanishadic teachings is the attainment of the unitive knowledge of Brahman. This knowledge is incompatible with rituals in any form, which naturally presuppose a distinction between the doer, the instrument of action, and the result. But the direct knowledge of Brahman can be attained only by a fortunate few who are altogether free of worldly desires and attachments and who have practised uncompromising discrimination and renunciation; the minds of average seekers are restless and attached to the world. One of the means of gradually acquiring inner calmness is ritualistic worship. According to Vedantic teachers, rituals, in order to be effective, should be accompanied by meditation. Meditative worship, called upasana, is directed to the Saguna Brahman, that is to say, the conditioned Brahman, or to any other deity approved by the scriptures. Upasana is described as a mental activity; the mind of the worshipper should flow without interruption toward the object of worship.

Upasana produces two kinds of results: seen and unseen. It may lead to the knowledge of the deities and enjoyment of material happiness. It may also lead to introspection and finally to liberation. The spiritual value of upasana depends upon the motive of the worshipper; the less selfish his mind is, the better fitted it is for the acquisition of concentration, without which deep spiritual truths cannot be realized.

According to some Vedic scholars, for instance Sayanacharya, upasana may be directed either to the Brahman with attributes or to a material symbol called pratika. Since the attributeless Absolute is still beyond his comprehension, the advanced student meditates upon Brahman associated with attributes, described in one of the Upanishads as He "whose creation is this universe, who cherishes all desires, who contains all odours, who is endowed with all tastes, who embraces all this." The upasana associated with material symbols is prescribed for the less advanced seekers, who, on account of their strong attachment to physical objects, cannot think of the attributeless Brahman. One kind of symbol is an accessory of the sacrifice, but such symbols have now become obsolete on account of the disappearance of the Vedic sacrifices. Another kind is a physical object on which the idea of Brahman or a deity is superimposed; it is worshipped as a representative of the deity or as Brahman. The Upanishads also speak of such symbols of Brahman as the mind, the sun, the wind, and the word *Om*.

The mechanical performance of rituals without meditation has very little immediate spiritual value; but as already stated, rituals are conducive to deeper concentration, which has a real spiritual significance. The highest tangible result of upasana (ritual with meditation) is the attainment of Brahmaloka, where one enjoys the most exalted form of phenomenal bliss. By means of upasana, however, a sincere worshipper can gradually sublimate his desires for gross objects. Upasana also trains the mind, naturally confined to the limited, to comprehend the vast. Thus the Upanishads, whose sole purpose is to inculcate the knowledge of Brahman, prescribe various forms of rituals associated with meditation as necessary steps for the attainment of such knowledge.

Though the Vedic rituals have now disappeared from India, yet the principles underlying them have been preserved, nay expanded, in the later scriptures, which deal mostly with bhakti or love of God as an effective spiritual discipline. The source of the bhakti doctrine is to be found in the Vedic upasana, self-surrender being the ultimate goal of both.

The physical symbols used in the popular religion of modern India are classified into two groups; either they may be natural objects such as a tree, the sun, a river, fire, or a special piece of stone, or they may be images or pictures. These symbols remind the devotees of certain aspects, powers, and attributes of the Godhead. The symbol is not the Godhead; through it one contemplates the Godhead. All worship and contemplation, in so far as they are mental activities, are symbolic. To see God everywhere and to practise the presence of God uninterruptedly is not possible for the beginner. So he is asked to see God wherever there is a manifestation of His power, splendour, beauty, and love.

There is another kind of worship in modern India, which is associated with God's incarnations on earth. There is no essential difference between God and His incarnation; Krishna, Rama, and other incarnations are worshipped by their respective devotees for the fulfilment of worldly desires and also for the purpose of obtaining salvation.

Hindu teachers say that the spiritual life begins with symbolic worship but in the end such worship is transcended. According to the Puranas, to see God everywhere, naturally and spontaneously, represents the highest spiritual stage; meditation comes second; in third place is worship through symbols; and fourth is the performance of rituals and pilgrimage to sacred places. According to another text, worship through images is the lowest, the next higher is the recital of mantras and the offering of prayers, superior to that is mental worship, and the highest of all is contemplation of the Absolute. The adept sees God everywhere; but the weaker devotee requires a concrete support. As the pilgrim makes his progress, he goes from the lower to the higher form of worship. After reaching the goal, he sees the same Godhead everywhere—in images, stones, nature, in all living beings, and in his own heart.

The most common objects of worship among the Hindus are human representations of the supreme spirit in the form of images. As long as the worshipper regards himself as a human being, he finds it easier to commune with a humanized God. Such a God can listen to prayers, answer them, and accept worship. Men can love Him and receive His love in return. Worshippers generally establish a definite relationship with the Deity, regarding Him as Master, Father, Mother, Friend, Child, or Beloved. There are two main types of humanized God: male and female. Brahma, Vishnu, and Siva are the most important male deities. Rama, Krishna, and Nrisimha (half lion and half man) are some of the divine incarnations worshipped by the Hindus; Kartikeya, a son of the Divine Mother, and the embodiment of valour, is highly venerated in South India. Besides these, there are other male deities, such as Ganesha, the god with an elephant's head, and Hanuman, the monkey chieftain. Such female deities as Kali and Durga represent the Sakti, or creative power, of Brahman. Brahman and its power are inseparable. Innumerable are the deities embodying the diverse attributes and powers of the spirit. Worship may be offered to any of the symbols, for it ultimately reaches the supreme Godhead, which alone bestows upon devotees the fruit of their prayer, either in the form of worldly happiness or of supreme liberation.

Rituals help to create a religious climate, and also often express the devotee's exuberance of sentiment at a particular stage of his spiritual development. They heighten a man's devotion to the Lord. Though rituals differ in different parts of India and also with regard to different gods and goddesses, there is an underlying similarity. Images are worshipped in the houses of those who can afford such worship, and also in temples. The deity is treated as an honoured guest, especially in the home, and in the temple as the King of kings. In the paragraphs immediately following is a description of ritualistic worship such as may be seen anywhere in India.

Though Hinduism stresses mental worship, it encourages as well external worship with physical ingredients, especially for beginners. In the mental worship the devotee regards the heart as the seat of the Deity, whom he conceives as having a luminous body. All the articles of worship, such as flowers, lights, incense, food, and water, are mental. In the external worship the devotee takes the spirit-form of the Deity from his heart and places it on the image before him, which has been decorated with flower garlands, looking upon the image as the living God. The mode of worship is like that of the service usually rendered to a beloved guest or to an honoured king. The devotee washes the feet of the image and makes offerings of sandal paste and rice grains as a mark of respect. He puts a sacred thread on the image, offers flowers made fragrant with sandal paste, burns incense, waves a lamp, offers food, and makes a gift of gold. Before bidding the Deity farewell, he performs a special ritual with a lamp, lighted camphor, conch shell, flower, and fan. The ceremony over, the worshipper takes back the spirit-form from the image and reinstalls it in his own heart, its real dwelling-place.

In the temples the priest attends on the Deity as on a king. Early in the morning he arouses the Deity from sleep with music, and after giving him a ceremonial bath, dresses him in royal robes and decks him with ornaments and flowers. He waves lights before him and offers him food and drink. Then the Deity holds court, giving audience to devotees, hearing their complaints, and granting their prayers. On festive occasions he is taken in procession with all the regalia befitting an emperor.

This is, in short, the popular religion practised by a pious Hindu. But through all these rituals and forms the worshipper does not forget the absurdity of trying to gratify the spirit by means of perishable offerings. Hence he prays to the Deity: "O Lord, in my worship I have attributed forms to Thee, who art formless. O Thou teacher of the world, by my hymns I have, as it were, contradicted Thy indescribable nature. By going on pilgrimage I have, as it were, denied thy Omnipresence. O Lord of the universe, pray, forgive me these three transgressions."

To complete the description of the usual religious life of a

Hindu, mention may be made of festivals, purificatory fasts, birthdays of saints, and pilgrimages to holy places.

Religious festivals are frequent in India. On these days Hindus often observe fasts and offer special worship. Many of these festivals commemorate certain events in Hindu mythology which symbolize the destruction of the forces of evil by those of good; a popular festival in North India, called the Ramalila, depicts the destruction by Rama of the wicked monster-king Ravana. Festivals are colourful occasions giving rise to innocent joys and merriments, and offering relief from the humdrum chores of daily life. Fasting gives inner purity; the feasting which follows develops the social sense. Different days are set apart for this purpose for the devotees of different cults. Sometimes devotees keep vigil for the whole night, reading from the scriptures and worshipping God; special worship is offered on the birthdays of the great religious teachers and mystics who were the creators of India's spiritual culture. Pilgrimages are made to holy places, the pilgrims practising austerities and often walking on foot great distances into almost inaccessible regions. Pilgrimages quicken the devotee's spiritual life. Often spiritual aspirants practise austerities in these places and attain to the vision of God, thus intensifying the holy atmosphere.

Rituals and myths, besides quickening the spiritual life of the Hindus, have enriched India's art, architecture, and literature. Temples, priests, and pilgrimages have kept Hinduism alive through the dark periods of her history. With the help of concrete worship many have attained great spiritual depths. Even what is regarded as crude and superstitious in the popular worship often reveals the genuine fervour of the worshipper. A Christian missionary has described how one day, near the Elephanta Cave at Bombay, he saw a primitive man absorbed in worship. The uncouth man was seated by the roadside before a phallic symbol of Siva. The disgusted missionary, coming near, saw a sudden light on the face of the worshipper and exclaimed: "Ah, after all, in spite of his superstition, he has it. But with all my education I am still in the dark." [1] It is amazing to see how many saints have been produced by Hinduism, Roman Catholicism, and Mahayana Buddhism, all rich in rituals and mythology.

Through religious festivals, pilgrimages, the observance of vows, and ritualistic worship, a Hindu cleanses his heart, renews his contact with God, and makes progress toward his spiritual goal. The perfect man, of course, regards every moment as holy, every action as service to God, every thought as communion with the Deity. But this goal cannot be reached without hard discipline. Only when the seeker transcends the duality of the phenomenal world and realizes his oneness with ultimate reality does he transcend rituals and concrete worship. This is evidenced in the following Hindu hymn:

How can one invoke the all-pervading Absolute?
How give a seat to that which is the sole support of all?
How can one bring offerings to that whose nature is pure awareness,
Or purify that which is ever pure?

Why should one bathe with water that which is utterly free from stain,
Or offer clothes to that which folds the universe in itself?
Why place a sacred thread on Him who has no bodily form?
Why offer fragrant flowers to one indifferent to smell?
How can perfume be pleasing to Him who is totally unattached,
Or jewels set off the beauty of Him who is all beauty's source?
Useless are gifts of food to one who is ever satisfied.

[1] About the much misunderstood phallic symbol, it may be noted here that just as a Christian, in partaking of holy communion, does not feel that he is behaving like a cannibal, so a Hindu, in worshipping Siva, does not think of sex or procreation.

*How can one circumambulate Him who is boundless in all
   directions,*
*And how contrive to salute Him who is one and without a
   second?*
*How can hymns be pleasing to that which the Vedas cannot
   reveal?*
How can one wave lights before the self-illumined Lord?
How install an image of one complete within and without?

Perfect knowers of Brahman, always and under all conditions,
Worship the Lord by knowing their total identity with Him.

XI.

Interreligious Relations: A Hindu Attitude

FROM the time of the Vedas, the earliest recorded history of India's spiritual culture, to that of Ramakrishna, the prophet of modern India, Hinduism has shown goodwill and respect for other religions. Despite sporadic instances of sectarian intolerance, the history of India is singularly free from religious strife. Even before the Christian era, India afforded shelter to a Jewish group, which was given freedom to pursue its own form of worship. Thomas, one of the apostles of Christ, came to India to preach the gospel of his master, and established a church in South India which is still functioning. Most of the Parsis, when persecuted in their homeland, came to India, where they are living today as the remnant of the grand ancient Zoroastrian faith. Hindu kings frequently helped the Moslems to build their mosques, in spite of the fact that the Moslem rulers of India often destroyed Hindu temples, disfigured Hindu images, and converted the Hindus to their faith often by ruthless methods. The religious clashes between Hindus and Moslems that have occurred during the present century have been inspired largely by political factors, religion being used merely as a pretext.

The respectful attitude of Hinduism toward other religions can best be understood in terms of its philosophical basis. As has been explained earlier, ultimate reality, according to Vedanta, is Brahman, or the spirit, which is devoid of name, form, or attributes; and in the relative universe the highest manifestation of Brahman is the Personal God, who is worshipped under different names and forms by Hindus, Jews, Christians, and Moslems. A passage in one of the Hindu scriptures says: "Though without parts or attributes, Brahman assumes forms for the welfare of spiritual seekers." The Personal God leads devotees to the realization of the spirit. Though Buddhism does not officially recognize the Personal God, yet in actual practice the attitude of Buddhists toward Buddha is not very different from that of the votaries of other religions toward their respective prophets or saviours.

A religion which regards ultimate reality as impersonal truth, and at the same time recognizes the validity of its concrete manifestations for the benefit of struggling aspirants, cannot but admit the validity of all religious ideals and show them respect. The situation is quite different with those for whom the Personal God is the ultimate reality. To accept the doctrine of exclusive salvation and develop the concept of "either-or" are natural for them. Hinduism has never developed the theory of a jealous God or exclusive salvation; the idea of a chosen people is alien to it. In the Hindu monotheism all other deities are either absorbed in the supreme God or accepted as parts of Him, whereas in the Semitic monotheism they are not tolerated. The Bhagavad Gita says that people under the compulsion of desires, following their own natures, worship other deities with suitable rituals. The supreme God does not frown upon such worship; on the contrary, He deepens their faith in their respective ideals and enables them to obtain the object of their desires. The ultimate fulfilment of desires, however, comes from Him alone who is the real dispenser of the fruits of worship. To a disciple who criticized the questionable rituals of a certain Hindu sect, Sri Ramakrishna said that the members of that sect, too, if sincere, would enter God's mansion—it might be by the back door. Christ proclaimed that in his Father's house there are many mansions, and to emphasize the statement added that he would not have said so if it were not true. Vivekananda said that a man does not progress from error to truth, but from truth to truth—more correctly, from lower truth to higher truth. It cannot be that among sincere devotees of God some are in total error and some completely right. A man's spiritual life and method of worship are determined by his inner evolution. The Bhagavad Gita warns that the wise should not unsettle the understanding of the ignorant, but should instruct them, coming down to their level.

It is good to have been born in a church, but one should not die in a church. Religions as human institutions cannot be absolutely perfect, but God is perfect. Religion is not God, but shows the way to God. The teachings of any organized religion deviate somewhat from those of its founder. It is said that Satan was once asked how he would tempt a possessor of pure truth, and he replied that he would tempt him to organize it. As clocks should be corrected from time to time by the sun, so also religions. The correction is made by saints, who directly commune with God, and not by theologians, who are only interpreters of the scriptures.

As already stated, Hinduism, both at its source and during the period of its subsequent development, exhibits a remarkable spirit of catholicity. As early as the time of the Rig-Veda it was said: "Reality is one; sages call it by various names." We read in an Upanishad: "May He, the One without a second, who, though formless, produces by means of His manifold powers various forms without any purpose of His own; may He from whom the universe comes into being at the beginning of creation and to whom it returns in the end—endow us with good thoughts." Again: "As flowing rivers disappear in the sea, losing their names and forms, so a wise man, freed from names and forms, attains Brahman, who is greater than the great." One cannot distinguish a Hindu from a Moslem, nor a Christian from a Jew, when they are absorbed in the infinite spirit. One sees differences only on a lower level, but from the summit all distinctions disappear.

That the non-dual spirit is worshipped under different names is reiterated by Hinduism. Here is a text from a Hindu scripture: "May the Lord of the universe, the remover of evil —whom the devotees of Siva worship as Siva, the Vedantists as Brahman, the Buddhists as Buddha [and, we may add, the Christians as the Father in heaven, the Jews as Jehovah, the Moslems as Allah], the followers of the Nyaya philosophy who are clever in logic as the Divine Agent, those devoted to the Jaina doctrines as Arhat, the ritualists of the Mimamsa school as karma—grant us all the desires of our hearts."

That all paths lead to the same goal is emphasized in the following hymn: "Different are the paths laid down in the Vedas, in Samkhya, in Yoga, and in the Saiva and Vaishnava scriptures. Of these, some people regard one and some another as the best. Devotees follow these diverse paths, straight or crooked, according to their different tendencies. Yet, O Lord, Thou alone art the ultimate goal of all men, as the ocean is the goal of all rivers."

As noted in a previous chapter, Hinduism itself provides for more than one divine incarnation. A good Hindu shows respect to them all, and to those believed in by other religions as well. It is related that when at one time Arjuna extolled Krishna, who was of a dark complexion, as the unique avatara, Krishna asked his disciple to follow him, and they entered a forest. Krishna pointed out to Arjuna a big tree and asked him if he knew what kind of tree it was. After observing it, Arjuna said that it was a blackberry tree with clusters of berries hanging from it. But coming nearer, Arjuna discovered that they were not berries at all, but innumerable Krishnas hanging from the Tree of the Absolute. Krishna, Buddha, Christ, and the other incarnations are so many waves in the ocean of existence-knowledge-bliss absolute.

One day Ananda, the foremost disciple of Buddha, said to his master that Buddha was the greatest of all the prophets of the past, present, and future. Thereupon Buddha asked the disciple whether he knew of all the prophets that had been born in the past since the creation, and of all the prophets that would descend on earth in the future till the world came to an end, and even whether he knew of all the godlike men who were living in different parts of the earth at the present time. Ananda was ashamed of his dogmatism.

According to Hinduism, no prophet is unique in the sense that he is the greatest of all. All receive their message from the one source and present it to men to suit their particular needs. In the teachings of Christ, Buddha, Mohammed, Krishna, and Moses one may see apparent differences due to the peculiar requirements of the people whom these prophets taught. But in their communion with reality they all experienced the same goodness, beauty, and truth. The common inner experiences of prophets are not noticed by their followers; the apparent external differences in their teachings account for much of religious quarrelling and controversy.

The harmony of religions found its most vivid expression through the spiritual experiences of Ramakrishna. This saint of modern India practised all the dualistic and non-dualistic disciplines of Hinduism and always arrived at the same state of God-consciousness. He pursued the teachings of Christ and Mohammed, and attained the same spiritual goal. One notice-able feature of his spiritual practices is that when he followed a particular path, he became completely absorbed in it and forgot everything else. While pursuing Islamic disciplines, he ate, dressed, and acted like a Moslem, removed the pictures of the Hindu deities from his room, and stopped going to Hindu temples. Thus he taught from actual experience, and not from mere book knowledge, that all religions are but different paths to reach the same goal. He also taught that a devotee of any faith need not give up his own rituals or beliefs, for he will certainly realize God with their help if he is sincere.

One of his favourite songs was the following:

I have joined my heart to Thee: all that exists art Thou.
Thee only have I found, for Thou art all that exists.
O Lord, Beloved of my heart! Thou art the home of all;
Where indeed is the heart in which Thou dost not dwell?
Thou hast entered every heart: all that exists art Thou.
Whether sage or fool, whether Hindu or Mussulman,
Thou makest them as Thou wilt: all that exists art Thou.

Thy presence is everywhere, whether in heaven or in Kaaba;
Before Thee all must bow, for Thou art all that exists.
From earth below to highest heaven, from heaven to deepest earth,
I see Thee wherever I look: all that exists art Thou.
Pondering, I have understood, I have seen it beyond a doubt:
I find not a single thing that may be compared to Thee.
To Jafar it has been revealed that Thou art all that exists.

Ramakrishna often described different religious experiences as different melodies of music. One day, as he listened to a concert, he said to a religious leader who was intolerant of religions other than his own: "Do you hear how melodious that music is? One player is producing only a monotone on his flute, while another is creating waves of melodies in different modes. Why should I produce only a monotone when I have an instrument with seven holes? Why should I say nothing but, 'I am He, I am He'? I want to play various melodies on my instrument with seven holes. Why should I say only, 'Brahma! Brahma!'? I want to commune with God through various relationships—sometimes regarding myself as His servant, sometimes as His friend, sometimes as His mother, and sometimes as His sweetheart. I want to make merry with God. I want to sport with God."

On another occasion, addressing some members of a religious sect who believed only in a formless God, he said:

We are all calling on the same God. Jealousy and malice need not be. Some say that God is formless, and some that God has forms. I say, let one man meditate on God with form, if he believes in form, and let another, if he does not believe in any form, meditate on the formless Deity. What I mean is that dogmatism is not good. It is not good to feel that my religion alone is true and other religions are false. The correct attitude is this: my religion is right, but I do not know whether other religions are right or wrong, true or false. I say this because one cannot know the true nature of God unless one realizes Him.

Hindus, Moslems, and Christians all seek the same object. A mother prepares dishes to suit her children's stomachs. Suppose a mother has five children and a fish is bought for the family. She does not prepare pilau or fish curry for all of them. All have not the same power of digestion. But she loves all her children equally. Do you know my attitude? I like all the preparations of fish. I feel quite at home with every dish—fried fish, curried fish, pickled fish. And what is more, I equally relish a rich preparation like pilau.

Do you know what the truth is? God has made different religions to suit different aspirants, times, and countries. All doctrines are so many paths; but a path is by no means God Himself. Indeed, one can reach God if one follows any of the paths with whole-hearted devotion. Suppose there are errors in the religion that one has accepted; if one is sincere and earnest, then God Himself will correct those errors.

If there are errors in other religions, that is none of your business. God, to whom the world belongs, takes care of that. The view that you hold is good indeed. You describe God as formless. That is fine. One may eat a cake with icing, either straight or sidewise. It will taste sweet either way.

But dogmatism is not good. You have no doubt heard the story of the chameleon. A man entered a wood and saw a chameleon on a tree. He reported to his friends, "I have seen a red lizard." He was firmly convinced it was nothing but red. Another person, after visiting the tree, said, "I have seen a green lizard." He was firmly convinced it was nothing but green. But the man who lived under the tree said: "What both of you have said is true. The fact is, however, that the creature is sometimes red, sometimes green, sometimes yellow, and sometimes has no colour at all."

God has been described in the Vedas as both with form and without. You describe Him as without form only. That is one-sided. But never mind. If you know one of His aspects truly, you will be able to know His other aspects too. God Himself will tell you all about them.

The harmony of religions, as preached by Ramakrishna, fulfils a pressing need of the times. Due to science and technology the world has shrunk, as it were, and human beings have come closer together. Since religion is a vital force in men's lives, how can there be peace in the world unless the different religions show mutual respect and work for the common good of humanity? In the past religions have produced both good and bad results. On the one hand, they have contributed greatly toward peace and progress, building hospitals and charitable institutions, promoting art and literature, and conferring many other blessings upon humanity; on the other hand, in the name of religion people have waged war, persecuted their fellow beings, and destroyed monuments of human culture. There are enough religions in the world today to give men the incentive to hate one another, but there is not enough of the religious spirit to inspire them to love one another. Indeed, religious intolerance has made many turn away from religion and seek solace in an ethical life, or in philanthropic work, or in the study of science and the humanities. Nevertheless it is not religion that is responsible for hatred and cruelty, but human bigotry and narrowness. And despite all the intolerance, there has always been an undercurrent of eagerness to promote interreligious amity. In discussing the Hindu attitude in this matter, we may briefly consider the following questions: Why are there so many religions? Where do they agree? Where do they disagree? What is the universal religion?

Let us take up the first question: Why are there so many religions? Different religions are differing forces in the economy of God, all working for the good of mankind; as we cannot destroy any force in nature, so we cannot destroy any of these spiritual forces. Different faiths are necessary to suit the diversity of human temperaments. Some men are emotional, some rational, some introspective, some active; again, there are those who wish to contemplate an abstract ideal, and those who wish to worship through concrete symbols. If there were only one religious discipline, there would be no hope for those who did not respond to it. Hence it is fortunate that there are many religions instead of only one, as many would prefer to have it. The greater the number of religions, the more chances people will have to satisfy their spiritual hunger. If there are different restaurants in a city, everyone will have an opportunity to choose the food that is most suited to his taste and requirement. People can get the same nourishment from rice, bread, or potatoes; the same illumination comes from lamps of different shapes, and the same white milk from cows of different colours. Religion will not have fulfilled its mission until every man has evolved his own religion, revealing to him his unique relationship with his Creator. If only one religion remained in the world, religion would be dead; variation is the sign of life, and always will be. Thinking beings must differ; difference is the first sign of thought. A thoughtful person prefers to live among other thoughtful persons, for the clash of thought stimulates new thinking. The very fact that all the great religions have survived till today proves that their utility is not gone. The religions of the world are not really contradictory or antagonistic; they are complementary. There is, in fact, no such thing as your religion or my religion, your national religion or my national religion; there is only one universal religion, of which all the so-called different faiths are but different manifestations. God is often described in Hinduism as the wish-reflecting gem. In Him everyone finds a reflection of his own ideal of truth, goodness, and beauty.

The different religions emphasize different facets of the supreme reality. Islam, perhaps more than any other religion, stands for the brotherhood of men among its own devotees. With the Moslems there are no social distinctions. It is inspiring to read about the pilgrimage of the Moslems to Mecca. There hundreds of thousands of the faithful discard their differing dress, whether of prince, ordinary citizen, or beggar, put on the seamless white garment which makes the chieftain indistinguishable from the shepherd, and proceed to the holy shrine to declare their surrender to almighty Allah. Before God all Moslems are equal. With the Christians, the central idea is: "Watch and pray, for the kingdom of heaven is at hand" —which means, purify your minds and be ready for the coming of the Lord. And one cannot but admire the love of God which innumerable Christians show through love of men, to whose service they devote their time, energy, and material resources. The idea of "sharing" is perhaps the most striking feature of Christianity in practice. Judaism has clung to the idea of God's power and justice, and the Jewish people with dauntless patience have faced the ordeals and sufferings through which they have passed for two thousand years without losing their faith in God's power and justice. Buddhism teaches how to attain peace through renunciation and service. In these days of selfishness and competition, it is a joy to see Buddhist monks serving people with infinite love and infinite compassion, as taught by their prophet. Hinduism makes the realization of God, who is both within and without, the central fact of life. Thousands of Hindus are willing, even today, to renounce everything—including the world itself—to experience the reality of God. Thus the different religions are like different photographs of the same building from different angles; and all of them are genuine pictures. Though people with vessels of different sizes go to a lake and carry away water, which takes the forms of the vessels, it is all the authentic water of the lake. And after all the vessels have been filled, the lake still appears to contain the same amount of water. None can exhaust the infinite power, beauty, love, and goodness of God.

Where do religions agree? In so far as religions belong to the realm of men's inmost soul, there are many remarkable similarities between them. The inner experience is the same everywhere; only the outer expressions are different, as determined by time and place. The end and aim of all religions is the realization of God, though the methods of realization may differ. The scriptures of the different religions merely point out different means to the attainment of freedom and universal love. All religions, in the words of Vivekananda, from the lowest fetish-worship to the contemplation of the Absolute, are so many attempts of the human soul to grasp and realize the Infinite, each determined by the conditions of its birth and association—and each of these marks a stage of progress; every soul is a young eagle soaring higher and higher, gathering more and more strength, till it reaches the glorious sun.

All the great religions, whether evolved in the regions of the Arabian desert or on the fertile banks of the Ganges, are founded on strikingly similar principles. They all believe in the existence of a soul which does not die with the destruction of the body, and in the reality of a God who is above nature and without beginning or end. Both Hinduism and the religions of Semitic origin believe in the original perfection of the soul; they also believe that men, by their own actions, have made themselves imperfect. But they all admit that souls will regain their perfection through knowing God. Saints and holy persons are objects of worship and veneration in all religions, and the Golden Rule is both implicit and explicit in all. All religions consciously or unconsciously exalt God's holy name and all claim to show the way out of the prison-house of this world. All exhort their followers to practise such spiritual disciplines as faith, prayer, self-control, and contemplation. The idea is implicit in the teachings of all prophets that the human mind can, at certain moments, transcend the limitations of the senses and of reasoning based upon sense-data, and come face to face with truth. So in many fundamental matters religions show striking similarity.

Where, then, do religions disagree? Here we must take into consideration certain fundamental factors which constitute an organized religion. Though the realization of God, or the attainment of perfection or freedom, is the ultimate goal, yet this can be achieved only by stages. At one stage religion emphasizes ritual, at another stage mythology, and at a third stage the doctrines and disciplines which constitute its philosophy.

Ritual, mythology, and philosophy may be considered the three important constituents of a well-organized religion. Mythology is the concretization of philosophy. It seeks to explain philosophy by means of the legendary lives of men or supernatural beings. Ritual is still more concrete. Bells, music, flowers, lights, images, and other concrete objects are freely used in ritual. But no agreement among religions can be established with respect to philosophy, mythology, or ritual.

Ritual has often been condemned by Protestant Christianity and Islam. Hinduism, the Mahayana Buddhism, and Roman Catholic Christianity recognize its importance, especially for beginners. A symbol, by the law of association, brings to mind the abstract ideal for which it stands. Music, it is well known, helps to concentrate the mind. Ritualistic worship, as described in the preceding chapter, helps to develop a devotional attitude. Some of the greatest saints of the world have been produced by religions rich in ritual and mythology—both of which have also contributed to the development of art, literature, and music. The stories of the fall of Adam and Eve, and of the Deluge, have important philosophical implications. Through various myths the scriptures try to explain abstruse truths. God' omnipresence, infinitude, or omniscience can scarcely be grasped by beginners in religion. And in spite of our intellectual attainments, most of us are only beginners.

Ritual, mythology, and philosophy are necessary factors in religious growth. Like husks, they protect the kernel of religious truth. The kernel is the essential part of a seed, but without the husk it cannot germinate. When the sprout appears the husk drops away. As one begins to dive deep in search of God, the non-essentials of ritual, mythology, and philosophy are discarded.

There is, however, no such thing as a pure religion. All faiths are conditioned by the three factors already mentioned, and all religious disagreements arise in these three fields. There cannot be any universal philosophy acceptable to all religions. When the followers of a religion regard its doctrines and disciplines as universal and desire others to accept them, a refusal on the part of the latter arouses ill-feeling, and sometimes human beings act like wild beasts. The same is true of mythology: when a religion claims that its myths alone are historical fact while those of others are pure superstition, misunderstanding and friction arise. In the field of ritual, the disagreement is just as pronounced: the followers of one religion may regard its own ritual as particularly holy, while declaring those of others to be arrant nonsense. Thus religious fanatics quarrel about non-essentials, fighting, as it were, over empty baskets while the contents have slipped into the ditch. Yet these non-essentials are necessary and must remain until men are firmly grounded in religious experience. As long as there exist different temperaments and needs, it will be impossible to find a universal philosophy, a universal mythology, or a universal ritual. Yet a universal religion is the dream of people who want to eliminate religious friction. What is this universal religion? Where does one find it?

Attempts have been made in the past to create a universal religion. There are the instances of Christianity and Islam, some of whose zealous leaders hoped to make their own faith into a universal religion. In order to impose it upon others they employed not only force of character, but more often bribery, persuasion, the sword, or a combination of all these. This desire in one form or other still persists, though history shows that a universal religion can neither be created nor imposed upon others in this way. Then people tried to formulate a universal religion, on an eclectic basis, by gathering together the non-conflicting ethical and other elements from the different faiths and eliminating those factors which give rise to friction. This intellectual method met with no better success, because religion is not a product of the intellect, but rooted in the direct experience of God by prophets and seers. Devoid of any roots, an intellectual religion withers away quickly, though it may look beautiful, like a bouquet of flowers of different colours picked from various plants. Attempts are often made to promote religious goodwill by means of interfaith breakfasts and luncheons, or by symposiums and discussions. All these functions stimulate the mind, but they do not go far.

As we have said, the universal religion already exists and needs only to be discovered. We do not see it because we emphasize rituals, mythology, and philosophy and ignore the basic truth. It is like universal brotherhood. We do not easily recognize this brotherhood because of our emphasis on racial and national prejudices. If we hold these in check we can see our brothers everywhere; but if we keep these prejudices intact and at the same time start organizing to promote human brotherhood, we only succeed in making confusion worse confounded. Human beings differ from one another in size, shape, and colour of skin, but an underlying humanity is common to all. One may not be able to lay one's finger on it, yet it exists all the same. Likewise the universal religion, in the form of God-consciousness, runs through all faiths, whether primitive, ethical, or highly mystical. The Lord says in the Bhagavad Gita: "I am the thread that runs through the pearls, as in a necklace." Each religion is one of the pearls. Through high philosophy or low, through the most exalted mythology or the most primitive and superstitious beliefs, through the most refined ritualism or the most stupid fetishism, every sect, every soul, every religion, consciously or unconsciously is struggling upward, toward God and freedom. Every vision of truth that a man has had is a vision of God and of none else. The Bible, the Vedas, the Koran, are so many pages in the scriptures of the universal religion, and an infinite number of pages remain yet to be unfolded.

The universal religion does not imply a set of universal doctrines or disciplines, nor a universal mythology, nor a universal ritual. Such a religion would be an impossibility, because of the diversity of human nature. The universal religion has no location in time or space. Its area is infinite, like the God it preaches. Krishna, Christ, Buddha, and Moses all have honoured places in it. Its sun shines upon all spiritual seekers: Hindu, Christian, Buddhist, or Moslem. In its catholicity this universal religion embraces in its infinite arms savages and civilized people, saints and sinners, philosophers and lovers of God, active men and contemplatives. There is no room in it for persecution or intolerance. Recognizing the potential divinity of all men and women it devotes its entire force to aiding men to realize their true divine nature. The real universal religion is not a creed or a doctrine; it is an experience. It is God-consciousness.

How are we to promote the universal religion? Let us recognize the fact that religions are complementary and not competitive. Saints and mystics have flourished in all religions; some such men have not belonged to any organized church. It is absurd to imagine that God is solely or even chiefly concerned with religion. Let us discard the idea of toleration, which carries with it a sense of superiority. Let us think of other religions in terms of respect and positive acceptance. A believer in the universal religion feels equally at home in a mosque, a church, a synagogue, or a temple. He sees his brother's face in a Moslem, a Christian, a Buddhist, a Jew, or a Hindu. He salutes all the prophets of the past, bows down before all godlike persons who are working today for the uplift of humanity, and keeps himself in readiness to show reverence to all the prophets of the future.

Let us encourage every man to dive deep into the mysteries of his own religion, and, provided he is sincere and earnest, he will one day discover for himself the universal religion.

In a circle with many radii, the farther we move from the centre, the greater will seem the distance between one radius and another. As we move toward the centre the distance will narrow down. At the centre all radii meet. The radii represent the different religions, and the centre is God. The farther we move from God, the greater will seem the difference between one religion and another. The nearer we are to God, the closer we shall feel toward other religions. In God we all meet. In order to promote religious harmony, let us deepen our religious consciousness. Let us come nearer to God by following our respective faiths, and not by jumping from one faith to another. Let the Hindu, the Moslem, the Christian, the Jew, emphasize the spirit and not the letter of their scriptures, and all religious quarrels will stop. Our religious edifice should keep all its windows open so as to permit fresh air from outside to come in; but we must not allow the wind to sweep the edifice off its foundation. The enemy of Islam is not Hinduism; the enemy of Christianity is not Judaism. All religions are challenged today by a common enemy: the rising tide of scepticism and secularism. If the religions do not hang together, they will hang separately. A Christian, to paraphrase the words of Arnold Toynbee, can believe in his own religion without having to feel that it is the sole repository of truth. He can love it without having to feel that it is the sole means of salvation. He can take Buddha's words to heart without being disloyal to Christ. But he cannot harden his heart against Krishna without hardening it against Christ.

In order to promote the universal religion we must not destroy other faiths. When a so-called civilized religion destroys, in the name of enlightenment, the beliefs and practices of a primitive people, it destroys something of their soul; religion is a part of the soul. We must not exterminate any faith, however crude it may be, nor superimpose our beliefs upon others; there must be no proselytism. By our own ardour and sincerity we may try to deepen people's faith in their own religions. Take a man where he stands and give him a lift.

To be sure, there will always remain differences in the nonessentials of religion. The world is a complex machine with intricate wheels. Let us try to make it run smoothly; let us lessen the friction by greasing the wheels, as it were. How can this be done? By recognizing the natural necessity of variation. Truth can be expressed in a hundred thousand ways, and each of these ways is true as far as it goes. And this expression of truth need not always be through a conventional theological God, but may use the medium of science, or art, or philosophy, or consecration to duty.

The preachers and ministers of religion have a tremendous responsibility in the promotion of world peace through the harmony of religions. It is to them that people look for guidance. How uplifting it will be if every church observes the holy days of other faiths! How effectively respect for other religions can be created if, for the scriptural reading, a minister selects passages from scriptures other than his own! How impressive it will be for the congregation if he tries to prove a point in his sermon by quoting from the words of prophets other than his own! People will then realize that religious experiences are universal phenomena and not the exclusive property of any one faith. This idea of exclusiveness always creates suspicion. A man with a sixth toe may be unique, but he is certainly not normal. When we begin by claiming superiority for our own religion, we end by asserting the superiority of our own interpretation of it. As Dr. Radhakrishnan has said, we start with the statement that Christianity is the best of all religions. Next we say that Protestantism is the best form of Christianity. Next, that the High Church is the true Protestant church. And lastly, that our own interpretation of the High Church is the best interpretation of the Christian religion.

Humanity is stricken today with a serious malady. This malady is essentially spiritual; political friction, economic unrest, and moral confusion are only its outer symptoms. Man is not at peace with his neighbours, with nature, with himself, or with his Creator. Greed, lust for power, and anger are abroad. Ill-will and suspicion are poisoning the very source of interracial and international relationships. The challenge of aggressive evil which is undermining human society can be met only by aggressive good. A drastic change in our thinking is imperative. Human nature shall have to be transformed. But this transformation can come neither through psychotherapy nor through science and technology, nor through military, political, or economic pacts. It is religion that can contribute in a large measure to bringing about the change. The great faiths of the world owe it to humanity to rise to the occasion.

As there are many dangers ready to engulf humanity, so also there are infinite possibilities to create a glorious world. Distance has been annihilated and men are now in a better position than ever before to compare notes with one another regarding their achievements and failures. Everyone has access to right knowledge and everyone can learn to make free use of it. In this fateful hour it is the duty of the religions to act as pointers to the goal of peace and freedom. Let them give tired humanity a song to sing. And let these mottoes be emblazoned on their banners: "Not destruction, but fulfilment," "Not condemnation, but acceptance," "Not dissension, but harmony."

APPENDIX

A Note About This Book

HINDUISM: ITS MEANING FOR THE LIBERATION OF THE SPIRIT was originally published in 1958 by Harper & Brothers Publishers, New York as part of its WORLD PERSPECTIVES series, planned and edited by Ruth Nanda Anshen. The present volume was number seventeen in the series. Other volumes in the series included the following:

World Perspectives

What This Series Means

IT IS the thesis of *World Perspectives* that man is in the process of developing a new consciousness which, in spite of his apparent spiritual and moral captivity, can eventually lift the human race above and beyond the fear, ignorance, and isolation which beset it today. It is to this nascent consciousness, to this concept of man born out of a universe perceived through a fresh vision of reality, that *World Perspectives* is dedicated.

Only those spiritual and intellectual leaders of our epoch who have a paternity in this extension of man's horizons are invited to participate in this Series: those who are aware of the truth that beyond the divisiveness among men there exists a primordial unitive power since we are all bound together by a common humanity more fundamental than any unity of dogma; those who recognize that the centrifugal force which has scattered and atomized mankind must be replaced by an integrating structure and process capable of bestowing meaning and purpose on existence; those who realize that science itself, when not inhibited by the limitations of its own methodology, when chastened and humbled, commits man to an indeterminate range of yet undreamed consequences that may flow from it.

This Series endeavors to point to a reality of which scientific theory has revealed only one aspect. It is the commitment to this reality that lends universal intent to a scientist's most original and solitary thought. By acknowledging this frankly we shall restore science to the great family of human aspirations by which men hope to fulfill themselves in the world community as thinking and sentient beings. For our problem is to discover a principle of differentiation and yet relationship lucid enough to justify and to purify scientific, philosophic and all other knowledge, both discursive and intuitive, by accepting their interdependence. This is the crisis in consciousness made articulate through the crisis in science. This is the new awakening.

Each volume presents the thought and belief of its author and points to the way in which religion, philosophy, art, science, economics, politics and history may constitute that form of human activity which takes the fullest and most precise account of variousness, possibility, complexity and difficulty. Thus *World Perspectives* endeavors to define that ecumenical power of the mind and heart which enables man through his mysterious greatness to re-create his life.

This Series is committed to a re-examination of all those sides of human endeavor which the specialist was taught to believe he could safely leave aside. It interprets present and past events impinging on human life in our growing World Age and envisages what man may yet attain when summoned by an unbending inner necessity to the quest of what is most exalted in him. Its purpose is to offer new vistas in terms of world and human development while refusing to betray the intimate correlation between universality and individuality, dynamics and form, freedom and destiny. Each author deals with the increasing realization that spirit and nature are not separate and apart; that intuition and reason must regain their importance as the means of perceiving and fusing inner being with outer reality.

World Perspectives endeavors to show that the doctrine of wholeness, unity, organism is a higher and more concrete conception than that of matter and energy. Thus an enlarged meaning of life, of biology, not as it is revealed in the test tube of the laboratory but as it is experienced within the organism of life itself, is attempted in this Series. For the principle of life consists in the tension which connects spirit with the realm of matter. The element of life is dominant in the very texture of nature, thus rendering life, biology, a trans-empirical science. The laws of life have their origin beyond their mere physical manifestations and compel us to consider their spiritual source. In fact, the widening of the conceptual framework has not only served to restore order within the respective branches of knowledge, but has also disclosed analogies in man's position regarding the analysis and synthesis of experience in apparently separated domains of knowledge suggesting the possibility of an ever more embracing objective description of the meaning of life.

Knowledge, it is shown in these books, no longer consists in a manipulation of man and nature as opposite forces, nor in the reduction of data to mere statistical order, but is a means of liberating mankind from the destructive power of fear, pointing the way toward the goal of the rehabilitation of the human will and the rebirth of faith and confidence in the human person. The works published also endeavor to reveal that the cry for patterns, systems and authorities is growing less insistent as the desire grows stronger in both East and West for the recovery of a dignity, integrity and self-realization which are the inalienable rights of man who may now guide change by means of conscious purpose in the light of rational experience.

Other vital questions explored relate to problems of international understanding as well as to problems dealing with prejudice and the resultant tensions and antagonisms. The growing perception and responsibility of our World Age point to the new reality that the individual person and the collective person supplement and integrate each other; that the thrall of totalitarianism of both left and right has been shaken in the universal desire to recapture the authority of truth and human totality. Mankind can finally place its trust not in a proletarian authoritarianism, not in a secularized humanism, both of which have betrayed the spiritual property right of history, but in a sacramental brotherhood and in the unity of knowledge. This new consciousness has created a widening of human horizons beyond every parochialism, and a revolution in human thought comparable to the basic assumption, among the ancient Greeks, of the sovereignty of reason; corresponding to the great effulgence of the moral conscience articulated by the Hebrew prophets; analogous to the fundamental assertions of Christianity; or to the beginning of a new scientific era, the era of the science of dynamics, the experimental foundations of which were laid by Galileo in the Renaissance.

An important effort of this Series is to re-examine the contradictory meanings and applications which are given today to such terms as democracy, freedom, justice, love, peace, brotherhood and God. The purpose of such inquiries is to clear the way for the foundation of a genuine *world* history not in terms of nation or race or culture but in terms of man in relation to God, to himself, his fellow man and the universe, that reach beyond immediate self-interest. For the meaning of the World Age consists in respecting man's hopes and dreams which lead to a deeper understanding of the basic values of all peoples.

World Perspectives is planned to gain insight into the meaning of man, who not only is determined by history but who also determines history. History is to be understood as concerned not only with the life of man on this planet but as including also such cosmic influences as interpenetrate our human world. This generation is discovering that history does not conform to the social optimism of modern civilization and that the organization of human communities and the establishment of freedom and peace are not only intellectual achievements but spiritual and moral achievements as well, demanding a cherishing of the wholeness of human personality, the "unmediated wholeness of feeling and thought," and constituting a never-ending challenge to man, emerging from the abyss of meaninglessness and suffering, to be renewed and replenished in the totality of his life.

Justice itself, which has been "in a state of pilgrimage and crucifixion" and now is being slowly liberated from the grip of social and political demonologies in the East as well as in the West, begins to question its own premises. The modern revolutionary movements which have challenged the sacred institutions of society by protecting social injustice in the name of social justice are examined and revaluated.

In the light of this, we have no choice but to admit that the *un*freedom against which freedom is measured must be retained with it, namely, that the aspect of truth out of which the night view appears to emerge, the darkness of our time, is as little abandonable as is man's subjective advance. Thus the two sources of man's consciousness are inseparable, not as dead but as living and complementary, an aspect of that "principle of complementarity" through which Niels Bohr has sought to unite the quantum and the wave, both of which constitute the very fabric of life's radiant energy.

There is in mankind today a counterforce to the sterility and danger of a quantitative, anonymous mass culture, a new, if sometimes imperceptible, spiritual sense of convergence toward world unity on the basis of the sacredness of each human person and respect for the plurality of cultures. There is a growing awareness that equality may not be evaluated in mere numerical terms but is proportionate and analogical in its reality. For when equality is equated with interchangeability, individuality is negated and the human person extinguished.

We stand at the brink of an age of a world in which human life presses forward to actualize new forms. The false separation of man and nature, of time and space, of freedom and security, is acknowledged and we are faced with a new vision of man in his organic unity and of history offering a richness and diversity of quality and majesty of scope hitherto unprecedented. In relating the accumulated wisdom of man's spirit to the new reality of the World Age, in articulating its thought and belief, *World Perspectives* seeks to encourage a renaissance of hope in society and of pride in man's decision as to what his destiny will be.

World Perspectives is committed to the recognition that all great changes are preceded by a vigorous intellectual reevaluation and reorganization. Our authors are aware that the sin of *hubris* may be avoided by showing that the creative process itself is not a free activity if by free we mean arbitrary, or unrelated to cosmic law. For the creative process in the human mind, the developmental processes in organic nature and the basic laws of the inorganic realm may be but varied expressions of a universal formative process. Thus *World Perspectives* hopes to show that although the present apocalyptic period is one of exceptional tensions, there is also at work an exceptional movement toward a compensating unity which refuses to violate the ultimate moral power at work in the universe, that very power upon which all human effort must at last depend. In this way we may come to understand that there exists an inherent independence of spiritual and mental growth which though conditioned by circumstances is never determined by circumstances. In this way the great plethora of human knowledge may be correlated with an insight into the nature of human nature by being attuned to the wide and deep range of human thought and human experience.

In spite of the infinite obligation of men and in spite of their finite power, in spite of the intransigence of nationalisms, and in spite of the homelessness of moral passions rendered ineffectual by the scientific outlook, beneath the apparent turmoil and upheaval of the present, and out of the transformations of this dynamic period with the unfolding of a world consciousness, the purpose of *World Perspectives* is to help quicken the "unshaken heart of well-rounded truth" and interpret the significant elements of the World Age now taking shape out of the core of that undimmed continuity of the creative process which restores man to mankind while deepening and enhancing his communion with the universe.

RUTH NANDA ANSHEN

New York, 1958